ON THE LAM

Lorna Poplak

ON THE LAM

Great (and Not So Great) Escapes from Prison

Copyright © Lorna Poplak, 2025

All rights reserved. No part of this publication may be reproduced, stored in a retrieval system, or transmitted in any form or by any means, electronic, mechanical, photocopying, recording, or otherwise (except for brief passages for purpose of review) without the prior permission of Dundurn Press. Permission to photocopy should be requested from Access Copyright.

Publisher: Meghan Macdonald | Acquiring editor: Kathryn Lane | Editor: Jess Shulman
Cover designer: Laura Boyle
Cover image: istock/erhui1979

Library and Archives Canada Cataloguing in Publication

Title: On the lam : great (and not so great) escapes from prison / Lorna Poplak.
Names: Poplak, Lorna, author
Description: Includes bibliographical references and index.
Identifiers: Canadiana (print) 20250220229 | Canadiana (ebook) 20250220237 | ISBN 9781459754379 (softcover) | ISBN 9781459754386 (PDF) | ISBN 9781459754393 (EPUB)
Subjects: LCSH: Escapes. | LCSH: Escaped prisoners. | LCSH: Fugitives from justice.
Classification: LCC HV8657 .P66 2025 | DDC 365/.641—dc23

We acknowledge the support of the Canada Council for the Arts and the Ontario Arts Council for our publishing program. We also acknowledge the financial support of the Government of Ontario, through the Ontario Book Publishing Tax Credit and Ontario Creates, and the Government of Canada.

Care has been taken to trace the ownership of copyright material used in this book. The author and the publisher welcome any information enabling them to rectify any references or credits in subsequent editions.

The publisher is not responsible for websites or their content unless they are owned by the publisher.

Printed and bound in Canada.

Dundurn Press
1382 Queen Street East
Toronto, Ontario, Canada M4L 1C9
dundurn.com, @dundurnpress

For my family

In prison, those things withheld from and denied to the prisoner become precisely what he wants most of all.

— Eldridge Cleaver

The administration of the Saint-Vincent-de-Paul Penitentiary was waiting for us. Why give a place of hatred and suffering the name of a saint who stood for love and charity all his life?

— French gangster Jacques Mesrine (*L'instinct de mort*)

CONTENTS

Introduction 1
1   Dead Man's Trousers 7
2   Smokescreens 17
3   Revisiting the Big House 29
4   High Flyer 45
5   Maximum Security 57
6   A Dog's Life 69
7   "Le Grand Gangster" 81
8   Marking Time 93
9   Fare and Foul 105
10   There Be Monsters 115
11   Porous Walls 125
12   "Run, Bambi, Run" 137
13   Blade Runners 147
14   Island Retreat 159
15   Unlawfully at Large 169
16   With a Little Help 177
Acknowledgements 187
Bibliography 189
Image Credits 203
Index 205
About the Author 213

Introduction

FREDERICK FERNANDO CADEDDU WAS THREE YEARS INTO A LIFE sentence for second-degree murder when a headcount at Millhaven Institution in Ontario on the night of May 25, 1980, revealed that he was missing. It would take hours for mystified prison authorities to work out exactly how he had engineered his escape.

After dinner that evening, as usual, the dirty cafeteria trays were stacked up side by side on stainless steel wagons and trucked off the prison grounds to be cleaned in the main kitchen facility at nearby Bath Institution. The difference on this particular evening was that the centres and inner edges of the plastic trays piled up on one of the wagons had been painstakingly cut out and the outer edges glued together to form a cavity, just large enough to fit Cadeddu's five-foot-seven-inch frame, curled up tight. The hollow stacks had then been topped with several intact trays to make his hidey-hole complete.

By the time kitchen staff discovered the empty container early the following morning, Cadeddu was long gone. He had grabbed a kitchen knife on his way out. Within hours, the Canadian public knew that an armed and dangerous murderer was on the loose.

///////////////

For as long as prisons have existed, people have tried to get out.

What, exactly, are they escaping from?

In the criminal justice sense, a prison is a building or complex for the detention of persons arrested or serving a sentence for an offence, but the concept has morphed over time.

Historically, primitive lockups in Canada were used simply to hold debtors or accused persons prior to the execution of their sentence. And the penalties were harsh: corporal or physical punishment such as flogging or branding, for example, most often carried out in a marketplace or similar public area for maximum effect, or capital punishment for an array of alarmingly trivial offences. In the early 1800s, a person could be condemned to death for stealing turnips, burning a stack of corn, or passing a counterfeit note.

The idea of imprisonment as punishment took hold in the late 1700s and early 1800s, and, in Canada, two types of institution emerged for the confinement of offenders.

The first is a jail (in earlier times, often spelled gaol), which operates on the local or provincial level for the detention of those awaiting trial, sentencing, or transfer to another facility, or with sentences of less than two years.

The second type of penal institution is a prison or penitentiary, run either on the provincial or the federal level and housing long-term offenders. As the name penitentiary suggests (think penance), there was originally a focus on repentance through isolation, silence, and oppressive doses of religious instruction, combined with hard, even brutal, labour.

What also arose were conflicting views as to the purpose of imprisonment. Punishment for crimes committed was important; just as important, if not more so, was the idea of deterrence. As a Select Committee prior to the establishment of Canada's Kingston Penitentiary put it in 1831: "It is quite enough for the purposes of the Public if the punishment is so terrible that the dread of repetition of it deters him from crime, or his description of it, others."

Rounding out the main goals of incarceration, although professional and public support for each of the four has seesawed over the years, are incapacitation, where the physical freedom of an individual is restricted for the protection of the public, and rehabilitation, where the objective is to make offenders fit to re-enter society at the end of their prison terms.

But, as emphasized by American criminal justice professor Richard Culp in a 2005 *Prison Journal* article, even though there may not be consensus on the primary end goal of imprisonment, another vital aim should always be kept in mind: "If there were such a thing as first principles in the field of corrections, the idea that prisons ought to prevent inmates from escaping would certainly qualify for the list."

How do you prevent inmates from escaping?

Some examples: fences, walls, lookout towers, barred doors and windows, guards surveilling inmates and monitoring pedestrian and vehicular entrances. Additional features, especially in maximum-security facilities for inmates regarded as dangerous, disruptive, or representing a flight risk, might include electrified fencing, barbed or razor wire on the ground or atop fences, armed patrols, canine units, closed-circuit television, and perimeter sensors — all designed to keep inmates inside.

And yet, as this chronicle of great (and not so great) prison escapes will show, these rigorous measures do not always deter determined individuals from attempting to get out.

The simple desire to be reunited with loved ones can spur on efforts to escape. Rudolph Nuss, one of fourteen men in a joint escape from Millhaven Institution, was recaptured after a week at his parents' home, and serial escaper (and mass murderer) Richard Blass, who broke free while being transported to a court hearing in Montreal, was found a few hours later hunkering down in his wife's apartment.

French gangster Jacques Mesrine escaped from the formidable stone Saint-Vincent-de-Paul Penitentiary in Laval, Quebec, which he described as a place of hatred and suffering. Raging against the appalling conditions, he returned to the prison thirteen days later in a well-organized attempt to foment a mass breakout.

Sometimes, escapes can be totally unplanned. Take Lionel Wright, for example. He joined a group of fellow inmates on the spur of the moment as they cut through the perimeter fence of a detention centre in Ottawa and scrambled into a waiting car. Wright would go on to become a member of the fabled Stopwatch Gang of bank robbers, who bedevilled Canadian and United States law-enforcement officers in the 1970s and '80s.

Desperation and a longing for freedom are great motivators. Apropos here is the case of Lawrencia "Laurie" Bembenek, who, after repeatedly being denied parole, broke out of a prison in Wisconsin and fled to Thunder Bay in Ontario.

And once again there is lifer Fred Cadeddu, who so spectacularly escaped from Millhaven hidden on a cafeteria cart in May 1980. While on the run, he took a bank manager hostage and robbed his bank in Hamilton, Ontario, of $101,000 before being recaptured and sent back to Millhaven in July of that year. "Foxy Freddie," as he was nicknamed by his admiring fellow cons, shared his thoughts with *The Toronto Star*'s Bob Graham in February 1981: "From day 1 in here I was thinking of getting out," he said quietly, adding, "No matter how much the public thinks that life in here is easy, with color [sic] TV, steaks, and all the other things, the bottom line is that there is no freedom to the outside world. And personally, that's what I think is the worst punishment of all."

The methods adopted by escapees range from the sensational, like Foxy Freddie's (or other examples such as fashioning ladders and clambering over walls, slathering on butter to squeeze between the bars, or decamping in a hijacked helicopter) to the mundane, like absconding during a transfer to court, hospital, or another correctional facility, or simply walking out the door.

///////////////

Although I hope that this anthology will prompt meaningful discourse on what the prison of the future should look like, the book is by no means a systematic treatise on carceral reform. Rather, the main focus of these sixteen chapters, loosely arranged in chronological order, is the age-old tug-of-war between prisons and escapees. Along with probing the origins, structure, and failings of a collection of historic and contemporary correctional institutions located largely, but by no means exclusively, in Canada, the stories highlight the attempts of masterminds, tricksters, villains, and innocents to claw their way to freedom — sometimes successful, mostly abortive, occasionally deadly.

The pages that follow flesh out the how, the where, the who, and the why of prison breakouts.

One thorny question, however, remains: What is the measure of a successful escape? As Dave St. Onge, historian and curator of Canada's Penitentiary Museum in Kingston, Ontario, puts it: Is it getting out or staying out?

1

Dead Man's Trousers

Ernest Cashel: Desperado on the Loose

ON NOVEMBER 19, 1902, D.A. THOMAS OF PLEASANT VALLEY, NORTH-West Territories (now Alberta), reported the mysterious and worrisome disappearance of his brother-in-law. Isaac Rufus Belt, a homesteader living in a shack on the Red Deer River to the east of Lacombe, had last been seen in late October in the company of a cattleman who called himself Bert Elseworth. Also missing were a saddle inscribed with Belt's name, his buckskin pony, his shotgun, a brown corduroy suit, and a significant sum of money, including a $50 gold certificate.

From descriptions of the man, police were convinced that Bert Elseworth was actually twenty-year-old Kansas-born Ernest Cashel. Described as a wild and reckless criminal, Cashel was a fugitive from United States justice. Although precise details of his early offences in his native land are sketchy,

Cashel, in a letter published by *The Weekly News Record* in March 1904, disclosed that drinking and gambling had led him into bad company, "and the first thing I knew I was looking out from behind the bars." After fleeing to the North-West Territories in mid-1902, he lost no time in resuming his felonious activities.

On October 14, a North-West Mounted Police (NWMP) constable arrested Cashel in Ponoka for forging a cheque. According to some reports, while Cashel was being escorted by train to stand trial in Calgary, he escaped by leaping off the train as it sped southward. Another more prosaic but probably more accurate version held that he made his escape by climbing out of the lavatory window as the locomotive steamed into the station at Red Deer. Eight days later, posing as Bert Elseworth, he stole a horse near Lacombe, and toward the end of the month he turned up at Belt's homestead.

The police suspected foul play when Belt disappeared, and the commanding officer of the NWMP's "E" Division in Calgary immediately dispatched ace investigator Constable Alick Pennycuick to seek out answers. After following several false leads, the tenacious policeman discovered in early January 1903 that a man named Elseworth had been busily, and illegally, acquiring possessions at different locations in the North-West Territories. He had "borrowed" a horse near Ponoka, as well as stealing a diamond ring in Kananaskis and clothing from a railway caboose in Canmore.

Then, on January 24, came the break that the police — and the nervous folks living in and around the little communities in the region — had been hoping for. A sharp-eyed station agent named W.L. Macdonald at Anthracite, near Banff, became leery of a "young fellow" who came into the railroad station that morning to cash a cheque.

As noted in a *Calgary Daily Herald* look back in May 1930, Macdonald told reporters: "My first glance at him aroused my suspicions. I knew that Cashel had a scar on the side of his forehead and this young fellow had his cap pulled down on one side of his face." After exchanging a few words with the stranger, then with the owner of the boarding house where he was staying, Macdonald became convinced that they finally "had the man who had terrified the country for weeks — people were afraid to open their doors to a stranger, the whole countryside was in a panic. I telephoned to the Mounties at Banff and found that Constable Blyth was on his way down to our town for a curling game."

There would be no curling for Blyth that day. On arrival, he arrested Cashel and escorted him to Calgary.

Police found the stolen diamond ring in Cashel's possession. As well, he was wearing a pair of brown corduroy trousers suspiciously similar to those of the suit belonging to the missing Rufus Belt. Tracing Cashel's movements, Pennycuick found that he had spent some time in November 1902 at an encampment near Calgary. There, the officer located a corduroy jacket that matched the pants. And, adding to the chain of circumstantial evidence tightening around Cashel, Pennycuick learned that Cashel had flashed a $50 gold certificate while staying at the camp.

But despite all that evidence, coupled with their grim suspicions, the police had no body; they had no tangible proof that Rufus Belt had been the victim of foul play. As a result, when Cashel appeared in court in Calgary on May 14, 1903, he was simply convicted for stealing the horse and the ring and sentenced to three years at the Stony Mountain Penitentiary (now Stony Mountain Institution) in Manitoba.

The situation changed dramatically in July, when a farmer living some fifty kilometres downstream from Belt's place spotted a body floating in the Red Deer River. Although badly decomposed, the corpse was positively identified from a foot deformity as being that of the missing man, Belt. Drowning was swiftly ruled out as the cause of death — Belt had been shot in the left side of his chest, and police recovered a .44-calibre bullet near his shoulder blade. This counted as another black mark against Cashel, who had been carrying a .44-calibre firearm at the time of his arrest.

The NWMP were convinced they had their man, and Cashel was returned to Calgary to stand trial for murder. Despite the vigorous defence mounted by Cashel's lawyer during his eight-day trial in October and the largely circumstantial nature of the evidence, the jury took just thirty-five minutes to return their verdict: Guilty.

The sentence: Death by hanging.

Hanging as the mandated punishment for serious crimes predated the existence of Canada as a country. It had been enshrined in law since the mid-1700s, when Britain imposed its criminal justice system throughout British North America. In the early days, more than a hundred offences were deemed heinous enough to warrant the death penalty. People could be hanged, for example, for burglary, arson, or robbing the mail. By the time the Confederation of Canada rolled round in 1867, however, there were just three crimes that merited the ultimate punishment — murder, treason, and rape.

With no recommendation for mercy from the jury, Cashel's fate was sealed. He would be held in a cell at the NWMP barracks guardroom in Calgary until his execution on December 15, 1903.

Wild rumours that a band of Cashel's supporters would sweep up from Wyoming (where he had been living prior to his flight to the North-West Territories) to spring him from jail had the police on edge, but, other than his spiritual adviser, Reverend G.E. Kerby, his only visitor was his twenty-four-year-old brother, John, who arrived from Wyoming in mid-November.

On the afternoon of December 10, as stated in an official NWMP report quoted in the May 1930 *Calgary Daily Herald* look back, "John Cashel came in, and, in direct violation of the orders governing his visits, walked to his brother's cell and stood talking to him with his hands on the bars." There were four guards on duty, including the unarmed death watchman, who was tasked with keeping the condemned man under constant surveillance. But there was a moment when three of them were bunched outside the cell and the fourth had his back turned to the prisoner. According to the report, although no one actually saw it happen, "it was at this critical moment John Cashel passed his brother two revolvers."

Around six o'clock that evening, as was required, the officer in charge ordered the death watch to take Ernest Cashel out of his cell so that the space could be thoroughly searched. Then the guards needed to frisk Cashel before locking him up again.

Before they could do so, as the report went on to explain, "the prisoner walked toward the door [of his cell] where the provost [officer in charge] stood and suddenly drew two revolvers from his trouser pockets. With these he at once covered the two unarmed constables. The armed constable, hearing some noise, foolishly walked up to the grating without drawing his revolver, and was confronted by the prisoner, who told him to put up his hands."

The hapless and helpless officers were ordered to drop their belts and weapons to the floor. They were then locked up in Cashel's cell. After collecting the keys from the provost's office down the hall to unlock his leg irons, Cashel kissed his hand to the guards in a cheery farewell gesture, assuring them blithely that he hadn't wanted to kill any of them but would have done so if he had to. He also told them that he had a horse waiting outside the building.

With that, he was gone.

It was, in a sense, a birthday gift to himself. According to a report in *The Globe* newspaper on December 11, he had turned twenty-one that day.

The night guard came on duty fifteen minutes later. He hastily released his fellows and sounded the alarm. But a fifteen minutes' start in the ferocious December blizzard that was now sweeping across the police grounds allowed more than enough time for Cashel to get clean away.

John Cashel was much less fortunate. Shortly after his brother's escape, he was arrested on a Calgary street clutching a package of boots and ammunition. If his intention was to pass them along to his brother, he must have felt bitterly disappointed.

The luckless guards who had allowed a dangerous criminal to break free did not escape the full weight of the law, either. All were subsequently court martialled, sentenced to prison terms, and dismissed from the force.

And so began a frenetic game of hide and seek.

As the Edmonton *Evening Journal* put it on January 25, 1904, the police were "stung by the taunts that they had become feeble upholders of the law and that the members of the force to-day had forgotten the traditions of the past."

Every available officer in Calgary joined the hunt, and reinforcements called in from Regina and Edmonton combed the whole of the southern North-West Territories. Members of the Blackfoot tribe assisted with the tracking.

G.E. Sanders, Calgary's superintendent of police, offered a $1,000 reward for the capture, or information leading to the capture, of Ernest

Cashel. In addition to a description (with details such as: "Figure, erect. Height, 5 ft. 8½ in. Weight, 145 lbs. Complexion, fair."), Cashel's "Wanted" poster offered other marginally useful snippets of information, such as the fact that his hair was "rather long over forehead, not quite as long as in photo" and that his face was "not quite so stout as in photo."

"Wanted" poster issued by the North-West Mounted Police after convicted murderer Ernest Cashel's escape from the Calgary barracks in 1903.

Once again, the countryside was wracked with fear. People living in the vicinity of Calgary were nervous. Farmers and ranchers barricaded themselves in their houses. There were sightings reported as far afield as Montana, which the U.S. authorities scrambled to investigate.

Conventional wisdom dictates that fugitives will try to put as much distance as possible between themselves and the place they've escaped from, but this is often not the case. It certainly wasn't so with Cashel. Throughout the whole period, he was never more than a few kilometres away from Calgary, and during much of the time he was in the city itself.

The Calgary police strongly suspected that the desperado had not left the area. Their suspicions were borne out by a confirmed visit near Calgary to the house of a rancher named Rigby, who was away at the time. Cashel stole a suit of clothes, leaving behind his old clothes and, as detailed in *The Wetaskiwin Times* on August 20, 1925, a nonchalant note saying: "Ernest Cashel, $1000, return in six months." Was this an IOU of sorts, a promise to come back and pay for what he had stolen? Given Cashel's well-documented record as a serial thief, it was more likely a brash boast.

On January 11, one month after his escape, Cashel robbed a farmer at gunpoint just east of the city, threatening vengeance if he were betrayed to the police.

The police believed that Cashel was keeping himself informed by reading the local newspapers, and they shrewdly persuaded the papers to stop printing stories about the case.

They also started putting together a posse. The group of men, made up partly of regular police officers and partly of civilian volunteers and members of the Canadian Mounted Rifles unit, was divided into squads of eight. With a focus on the eastern suburbs, the men were given instructions to search, as *The Wetaskiwin Times* put it in August 1925, "every building, cellar, root-house or haystack and to set fire to any such erections if it was necessary in order to force the fugitive out into the open."

One of the teams finally struck gold on a farm some ten kilometres from Calgary. A short distance away from the farmhouse, they found a "burrow" in a haystack containing items of clothing they recognized as belonging to Cashel. There was no sign of the man himself.

On searching the house, however, one of the officers was greeted with a revolver shot from the cellar, which, fortunately for him, missed its target. After an exchange of gunfire and several requests for Cashel to give himself up, the officer in command gave the order to torch the building. Moments later, Cashel, haggard and unkempt, emerged with his hands in the air.

On the way back to Calgary, Cashel became uncharacteristically chatty. He said that although he had had many opportunities to get clean away, he would not leave his brother, who had sacrificed so much for him. Ernest knew that John had been arrested, tried, and convicted, but not yet sentenced for abetting his escape, and that he himself was to be hanged on January 26 for the Belt murder.

Cashel also admitted to bearing a grudge against the man who had so relentlessly pursued him. A *Vancouver Daily World* report on February 2, 1904, quoted him as saying: "I wanted to kill Constable Pennycuick. I have been looking for him ever since I escaped."

On January 25, 1904, there were several interesting developments in what *The Calgary Herald* that day called "the most sensational case in the annals of Canadian crime."

First, John Cashel appeared in court to receive his sentence for assisting his brother in his escape. The judge had in hand a written recommendation for mercy from the jury, and, in addition, counsel for the defence made some forceful points in mitigation. To John Cashel's great relief, the judge decided to deliver a light sentence: "That the prisoner be confined in the common jail at Regina for a period of one year."

Half an hour later, Ernest Cashel, handcuffed and with an escort of five policemen, appeared in the same courtroom. As noted in a *Calgary Herald* look back in 1964, Cashel was informed that he had been given a week's reprieve, or, as the judge announced: "Ernest Cashel, you are given a reprieve from the sentence of this court from tomorrow until a week from tomorrow, Tuesday, February the second, and the sentence of this court is that you be taken back from whence you came, and on that date hanged by the neck until you are dead."

This postponement was granted not out of any consideration for the doomed man but to allow professional hangman John Robert Radclive sufficient time to get to Calgary from his home base in Toronto. Failing that, a certainly less-experienced local would have had to officiate, a possibility that the authorities shuddered to contemplate.

As for the $1,000 reward that had been offered immediately after Cashel's escape, Superintendent Sanders made it perfectly clear that no one need apply. All the public had done was provide vague suggestions as to Cashel's whereabouts (possibly because they were terrified at what might happen if they turned informer). It had taken a large-scale police hunt to capture the bandit.

As per an article in *The Weekly News Record* on March 3, 1904, Reverend Kerby, Cashel's spiritual adviser while he awaited execution, believed that his charge was not "wholly bad," as evidenced by the love he expressed for his mother and his clear affection for his brother. He had also lost his father while still in his early teens.

"It might have been different with me if I had had a father at this period of my life to have guided me. What possessed me of this wild spirit was having too much of my own way," Cashel told Kerby. Unexpectedly, he also faulted "dime novels [cheap, lurid paperbacks]. They filled my mind with wild and false notions of life."

But, he added, "I have no one to blame but myself for being here."

Ernest Cashel was hanged at the Calgary police barracks at 8:06 on the morning of February 2, 1904. Just before his execution, he confessed to the murder of Isaac Rufus Belt.

2

Smokescreens

How Norman "Red" Ryan Escaped from Kingston Penitentiary — Twice

AS THEY SCRAMBLED TO DOUSE A BLISTERING FIRE IN THE PRISON'S horse barn on September 10, 1923, the staff at Kingston Penitentiary had yet to discover that this was merely the sideshow; the main drama was being played out elsewhere. With clouds of billowing black smoke obscuring their movements, the five offenders who had planned and orchestrated this diversion quietly laid down their tools, slipped away from their work groups, propped a makeshift ladder against the wall, and prepared to climb over and out.

The cast of unsavoury characters consisted of bank robber Edward McMullen, burglar Andrew Sullivan, burglar and safecracker Gordon Simpson, Thomas Bryans, convicted of manslaughter, and, last but certainly not least, the undisputed ringleader of the group, career criminal Norman John "Red" Ryan. In a long and detailed report the following day, *The Globe* noted that the five convicts were serving terms of from ten years to life, adding dryly that they were certainly "not of the class that people would care to have go free."

Red Ryan (so-called for his shock of sandy red hair) was born in 1895 in west Toronto, one of eight children in a sprawling Irish Catholic family. He gave early notice of the devious path he intended to carve out for himself. At the age of ten, he started playing hooky from school. He was convicted of vagrancy in a magistrate's court and was bundled off to a reform school for Catholic boys. He escaped and was sent back.

His parents could not agree on what to do with troublesome Norman. His father, a violent and eccentric man, tried to whip the boy into compliance; his mother defended him. "For the adolescent Ryan," writes Peter McSherry in his comprehensive *The Big Red Fox: The Incredible Story of Norman "Red" Ryan, Canada's Most Notorious Criminal*, "it must have been a strange dichotomous world where he could be right and wrong at once." And, adds McSherry, "he must have learned early the value of a plausible story." As well as mastering the art of self-glorification, it would seem.

By 1908, Ryan — just thirteen years old — had convictions for bicycle and chicken theft. By 1912, his crimes had taken a more serious turn, and in December of that year he started serving a three-and-a-half-year sentence for burglary and shooting with intent to maim. An unforgiving magistrate sent him to Kingston Penitentiary (also known as Kingston Pen or KP), which would become his home away from home for long periods of his life.

Ryan was released from Kingston in 1914. Despite earnest protestations that he was done with crime, further convictions followed, the most serious being two twelve-year concurrent sentences for armed robberies, to be served in KP.

Ryan was saved from a long stretch in the penitentiary, however, when, in the dying days of the First World War, the Canadian government turned to conscription to bolster the country's war efforts. Even convicts were encouraged to enlist. The wily Ryan took advantage of this opportunity — which came with a full pardon.

He joined the Canadian Army on March 26, 1918, and was shipped off to England.

Ryan's six months as a soldier were punctuated by drunken brawls, a handful of robberies (shades of his youth, these included snatching chickens), and a period of absence without leave. His disreputable service ended with a court martial. After escaping from detention, he deserted.

Back in Toronto after a general amnesty in 1920, he seemed to go straight for a while, living with his family and working as a tinsmith. He was, however, leading a double life — appearing respectable but, in reality, engaged in increasingly violent armed robberies in Hamilton and Montreal. His luck finally ran out in 1921, when he was arrested in Montreal after a gun battle with police.

This time, Ryan would be in for the long haul.

In September 1922, he was found guilty on three charges of bank robbery and one charge of shooting with intent to maim. He was given a sentence of twenty-five years, and, once again, he found himself incarcerated in the Kingston Pen.

According to reports from informants, Ryan had no intention of remaining inside. In spite of increased vigilance from prison authorities, he enlisted the help of a coterie of lawbreakers both inside and outside the walls to plot his escape — these seemingly included some KP guards.

The plan came together at around 10:30 a.m. on September 10, 1923, with a blaze in the horse barn and a black pall that concealed five long-term convicts as they made a dash for freedom. By the time the alarm wailed and prison guards started firing wildly into the smoke, four of the men had already scrambled over the twenty-five-foot-high wall. Bringing up the rear with typical bravado was Red Ryan.

This violent and sensational escape sent shock waves through the community, and *The Toronto Daily Star* dispatched a hotshot young reporter, Ernest Hemingway, to cover the story. This was part of his melodramatic report: "As 'Red' Ryan started up the ladder, Matt Walsh, chief keeper of Portsmouth penitentiary, came running around the corner to see the burning barn. Walsh saw 'Red' on the ladder and ran toward the scantling [plank ladder] to try and jerk it down, shouting the alarm as he ran. 'Red' …

had left a pitchfork leaning against the jail wall for just this emergency ... Walsh tackled him and 'Red' swung with all his might on Walsh's head with the pitchfork. Walsh went down and 'Red' dropped the fork and went up the scantling and over the wall."

Ernest Hemingway was clearly honing his skills for his future career as a novelist.

One of Ryan's partners in crime didn't make it very far.

Instead of the powerful getaway car the escapees expected to find at their disposal, they were forced to settle for an old Chevy. Ed McMullen took the wheel. A prison guard armed with a rifle stepped in front of the rapidly accelerating vehicle and managed to take one potshot before leaping out of harm's way. The bullet smashed the steering wheel and tore through McMullen's right hand. Some six kilometres out of town, the car crashed into a farmer's field, and the convicts fled. At around 5:30 that evening, a prison official found McMullen lying beside a farm fencepost, weak from loss of blood.

For five days, the rest of the group lay low in the area, hidden and fed by a reluctant farmer. Despite a full-scale manhunt, they eventually managed to sneak into Toronto on September 16. On September 27, the "Red Ryan Gang" hit a Bank of Nova Scotia branch at the corner of Oakwood and St. Clair Avenues. After hastily dividing the proceeds of $3,107.22, the gang split up and left town.

Eager to get the hell out of Canada, Ryan and Andrew Sullivan hitched a ride to Windsor in a bootlegger's limo. Ryan later claimed that the duo had openly crossed the Detroit River aboard the Windsor ferry, with sawed-off shotguns hidden in their coats. According to McSherry, the truth was far less dramatic: they were smuggled into the United States on a rumrunner's launch.

For the next ten weeks, Ryan lived high off the hog in the U.S., wearing flashy clothes, sporting bling, staying in classy hotels, driving fancy stolen automobiles — and robbing banks. And he had earned the right to boast that he was now Canada's most notorious criminal.

By dint of monitoring Ryan's correspondence with his girlfriend in Toronto, a Canadian team tracked him down to Minneapolis, Minnesota. They enlisted the help of the local police, informing them that the fugitive would shortly be collecting his mail from the city's main post office. On December 14, Ryan was spotted at the post office and tackled by a squad of Minneapolis detectives. After being shot in the shoulder during an exchange of gunfire, he was taken into custody.

Ryan fought extradition to Canada from a cell in the Minneapolis City Jail, seemingly preferring a shorter prison term for the crimes he had committed in the U.S. to the certain twenty-five-year or life sentence that awaited him at home. Perhaps his real aim was to escape from the jail by sawing through the bars of an outer window and climbing through, for when hacksaw blades and a homemade rope were discovered on his person, he gave up his efforts to remain in the States.

Shackled hand and foot and escorted by a bevy of policemen, Ryan was extradited to Canada in January 1924.

His future looked grim.

////////////////////

Time magazine dubbed him "Ryan the Prodigal," and with good reason.

Back in the Pen with a life sentence, Norman Ryan underwent an amazing transformation. Mentored by the prison chaplain, Wilfrid T. Kingsley, he rediscovered his Catholic roots. He delivered thunderous addresses advising fellow inmates that "crime doesn't pay." Prison reform societies, various press outlets (notably, *The Toronto Daily Star*), and even politicians, including Conservative Prime Minister R.B. Bennett, were beguiled by his charisma and apparent sincerity. Despite strident Liberal Party demands for a Royal Commission to investigate conditions in Canadian prisons, many believed the conversion of this hardened bank robber proved that the correctional system was not so bad after all.

Concealed behind all Ryan's endeavours was his Plan A: to get out of prison. There was no Plan B.

And, astoundingly, it all worked out very well.

On July 23, 1935, KP's warden, Richard Allan, despite deep misgivings, informed Ryan that he was to be released — not through the normal process (as a lifer, a repeat offender, and a person who had committed at least one major crime, he was well and truly disqualified) but through the personal intervention of the prime minister. He had been issued a ticket of leave, which entitled him to be paroled with minimal oversight, other than Father Kingsley's supervision and a monthly report to the police in his hometown, Toronto.

In spite of his record of nineteen convictions for theft and violence and at least nine gun battles with police or the public, as well as his life sentence at a time when life really did mean spending the rest of your days shut up in prison, Ryan, after serving just eleven and a half years, was a free man.

As he stepped through KP's North Gate, clad in a new brown suit and with his prison pay clinking in his pocket, did his mind flash back to that very different exit in September 1923, when he and his four fellow-long-haulers scrambled over the wall in a cloud of smoke to the wailing of the alarm and the crackle of gunfire?

Impossible to know.

What we do know is that shortly after his release, as *The Toronto Daily Star* shared with its readers on July 25, 1935, Ryan spoke movingly of his past life: "What a fool I was — anyone is, too, who thinks crime reaps a dividend. Just one way — sorrow and remorse and a shattered life."

Before long, Ryan was working as official greeter and low-level manager at the Nealon House Hotel on King Street East in Toronto, with a salary of $50 a week. By January 1936, he was also selling Ford cars for Fawcett Motors in Weston. Ryan would speak freely about his past exploits, always swearing that he was done with "the foolishness of crime." As noted by McSherry, veteran crime reporter Gwyn "Jocko" Thomas once said: "Red had a nice smiling way about him. He was very charming."

The man had it made.

Shortly after his release, however, an alarming uptick in violent crimes sent several local police forces scrambling — some examples were a nighttime burglary at a Scarborough liquor store in October 1935, an attempted safe-breaking in December at the Bank of Commerce in Ailsa Craig, Ontario, and an armed robbery in April 1936 at a Bank of Nova Scotia branch in Lachute, Quebec, which netted the robbers $3,567.

The ghastliest crime of all took place in the early morning of Saturday, February 29, 1936. A shrill alarm alerted Edward Stonehouse, fifty-eight, and his twenty-four-year-old son, James, to a robbery taking place at their car dealership, located next to their home on Highway 7 in Markham, Ontario. After calling the local constable and grabbing their guns, they rushed over to the showroom to find thieves backing out in Edward's new car. Father and son jumped onto the running-board and managed to clamber into the vehicle.

As James told *The Toronto Daily Star* on the day of the robbery, "There were three shots. I knew they hit dad because he slumped over. I guess they either had a machine gun or a sawed-off shotgun. When my dad was slumped over I saw one of them hit him over the head with the butt of a gun."

The robbery was ultimately thwarted — after driving about four hundred metres in the stolen vehicle, the thieves abandoned it and made their getaway in another car — but at a terrible cost. Edward Stonehouse had taken a bullet to the head. He died on March 6 without regaining consciousness. James was shot in the stomach, and his right hand was shattered. He would die three years later, partly as a result of those injuries.

Ryan was vocal in his outrage at this heinous crime, and he reportedly offered to help the police crack the case. His proposal was politely refused.

///////////////

In May 1936, an armed robbery in the small port city of Sarnia, Ontario, brought the crime spree to a jarring and tragic end.

As described in *The Sarnia Canadian Observer* Centenary Edition of 1936, Sarnia was a "modern city of 20,000 souls … favored [sic] with an ideal location … the home of thriving industries … modern schools, churches, recreational centres and eight spacious parks."

What drew the robbers to the city, however, was not its top-notch amenities but the fact that the till at the local Liquor Control Board store would probably be stuffed with cash at closing time on the Saturday of the Victoria Day long weekend. Perhaps adding to the attraction was that the police department, numbering just thirteen men, was both understaffed and underfunded. Also, the officers were exceptionally poorly armed. The .32 Colt revolvers they carried were derided as popguns, certainly no match for the firepower of criminals of the day.

There were still twenty-five customers and staff in the liquor store at around 5:55 p.m. on Saturday, May 23, 1936, when two masked bandits dressed in blue overalls and railwaymen's caps locked the entrance door behind them and stormed into the shopping area, the bigger of them with a .38-calibre revolver in one hand and a .45 Colt automatic in the other. His companion, described as small and shrivelled, was armed with two .38 revolvers.

As *The Toronto Daily Star* informed its readers on May 26, the scrawny man then snarled, "This is a holdup."

With his accomplice covering the terrified customers and staff, the bigger gangster vaulted over a sturdy metal partition at the counter to scoop up the day's takings from the cash drawers.

An overview of the layout of the store will explain what happened next. The "in" and "out" doors at street level stood side by side, with the entrance on the left and the exit on the right, separated inside by a partition wall. The entrance took shoppers up a flight of stairs to the extreme left side of the shopping area. After making their purchases, they would move through to the right side, where another flight of stairs took them back down to street level. Usually, the exit was not accessible from the outside; that day, for some reason, the automatic closer of the door had been disabled.

So when two men, desperate to pick up a last-minute bottle, arrived at the store and found the entrance door locked, they simply sneaked in through the exit. After climbing up to the shopping area and taking in the scene at a glance, one of the latecomers silently slipped out to raise the alarm.

Within minutes, four armed police officers were en route from the police station in Sarnia City Hall, located some three hundred metres away. While one of the officers tried unsuccessfully to gain access through the entrance, the other three dashed in through the exit door.

By that time, the robbers were shepherding the customers and staff, their hands in the air, toward the back of the store. Hearing noises from the stairwell, the bigger gangster ran to investigate and was met by the trio of policemen, guns drawn.

The officer leading the group, Constable John Lewis, did not stand a chance. The bandit shot him four times at point-blank range. One of the bullets pierced an artery in Lewis's chest and he fell, mortally wounded.

Miraculously, neither of his fellow officers was hurt in the ensuing gun battle, but both robbers were brought down, trapped after trying in vain to flee through the entrance that, ironically, they themselves had locked. The little man, later identified as a small-time criminal named Harry Checkley, was dead within minutes of being transferred to the local hospital.

Thirty-three-year-old Constable Lewis died in hospital at about 6:45 p.m., with his wife, Vera, at his side. He left behind Vera and their two children, Donna, ten, and eight-year-old Jack. According to *The Toronto Daily Star* on May 26, 1936, Lewis's widow told the press when informed that her husband had led the charge: "Of course John would do that.... He was doing his duty; he wouldn't have thought of doing anything else."

The big man, shot in the head, arm, and ankle, would die at around 7:50 that evening.

On searching through his pockets, police found a driver's licence issued to John N. Ryan and a motor vehicle permit issued to Norman J. Ryan.

For the general public, the shock was complete. Not only had a police officer been mowed down in the line of duty in small, safe Sarnia, but his murderer was now revealed as Red Ryan, Ontario's criminous poster boy.

Photograph of Norman "Red" Ryan from *The Globe* of May 25, 1936, two days after he was mortally wounded during a bungled holdup at the liquor store in Sarnia. He would later die in hospital.

Photograph from *The Globe* of May 25, 1936, showing the bullet-scarred vestibule of the Sarnia liquor store where the robbery took place. Inset to the right is a picture of slain officer John Lewis, and at the bottom are the three officers who took down Red Ryan and his fellow bandit Harry Checkley.

In a withering article in *The Globe* on May 25, Harold Dingman wrote that "reformed public enemy" Ryan "was the victim of a trap sprung by his own stupid bungling in a petty hold-up of a liquor store. The last-ditch stand of Ontario's pet boy cost the lives of two others. Red shot a courageous young Sarnia constable ... in cold blood." And to what end? The sum of money that cost the lives of three men was "a paltry" $394.26.

Within days, thanks in part to information received from Ryan's brother Russ, Ryan was found to be implicated in the murder of Edward Stonehouse, the Lachute bank robbery, and several of the other cases that had kept police on the hop in late 1935 and early 1936.

For Ryan's supporters, the fallout was swift. As McSherry notes in *The Big Red Fox*, on being informed of Ryan's death, Father Kingsley, at first incredulous, later blurted out, "I dreaded something like that would happen." Overwhelmed by his protégé's duplicity, he tore up their correspondence and refused all interviews. Beneath the bold headline "'Glad he is Dead,' Say Mullins and Father Kingsley," *The Toronto Daily Star* revealed on May 26, 1936, that one of Ryan's keenest supporters, Senator H.A. Mullins, had frankly admitted that he had been "beaten" and "fooled." Now-former prime minister Bennett, who had been bundled out of office in the Liberal Party's landslide victory in the October 1935 general election, was quoted in the June 8, 1936, edition of *Time* magazine as saying curtly: "I feel the letdown very keenly."

But, as McSherry tells it, during the ten-month period between Ryan's release from prison and his death, not everyone had bought into his lies and sanctimonious self-aggrandizement. As early as July 1935, Ryan reportedly overheard a policeman chastising members of the press who had pushed so hard for his release: "Now *you've* let the beast out and, by geez, there'll be trouble." But the frustrated police feared challenging Ryan "because, of course, Ryan had powerful friends and a huge public image as a celebrated regenerate and paragon."

In a 1957 article for *Maclean's* entitled "Why Red Ryan's shadow still hangs over every prison yard," Ted Honderich underscores a grave long-term effect of the so-called paragon's cynical exploitation of the parole system in Canada. The year Ryan walked out of Kingston Pen, Honderich notes, 431 inmates received ticket-of-leave releases from federal institutions. Fourteen years later, the Canadian average per year was some 275, at a time where most other Western nations were increasing the use of parole to great effect. Honderich also quoted the blunt opinion of DWF Coughlan, director of Ontario's probation service: "The case of Norman Ryan put back the progress of parole in Canada by fifteen years. That one spectacular case did more against the system than the proven record of thousands of men has done for it."

"If I ever go in for crime again, I deserve to be shot," Ryan told *The Toronto Daily Star* back in July 1935.

Prophetic words.

3

Revisiting the Big House

Turning the Spotlight on Kingston Penitentiary

BY THE TIME RED RYAN AND HIS CREW USED THEIR SMOKE-AND-ladder trick in 1923 to escape from grim Kingston Penitentiary, that massive limestone structure had dominated Hatter's Bay (now Portsmouth Olympic Harbour) on Lake Ontario for just under ninety years.

On May 30, 1833, Lot No. 20, situated two miles west of Kingston and consisting of two hundred acres of land, was purchased for the purpose of constructing British North America's first true penitentiary.

The new prison would be modelled on a progressive penal philosophy, developed in the United States in the early 1800s. Under the Auburn system (also known as the social or silent system), prisoners worked during the day in a communal setting; at night they were confined in small, separate cells, with harsh discipline and complete silence imposed at all times. It was firmly believed that in addition to punishing offenders, this unforgiving regime, coupled with masses of religious instruction, was the surest path to repentance and rehabilitation. As a bonus, profits from the inmates' enforced labour would contribute toward the financial well-being of the prison.

Originally known as the Provincial Penitentiary of the Province of Upper Canada (now Ontario), the institution came under the federal umbrella after the Confederation of Canada in 1867, and its name was changed to Kingston Penitentiary.

From the outset, folks in Kingston were none too pleased with having this eyesore polluting their lakefront. As the local newspaper, *The Daily British Whig*, groused in 1834: "£12,500 have been expended in erecting a huge, unsightly and unfinished wing of an immense building ... all money gone."

That "huge, unsightly and unfinished wing" was the south wing, containing 144 cells in five tiers. Although as part of a major reconstruction starting in 1890 the cells were increased in size and equipped with plumbing and electricity, those dark, back-to-back, airless chambers originally measured eight feet in length and twenty-eight inches in width. Just enough room for a bed that could be folded up when not in use and a bucket for waste.

It would take until 1861 for construction of the main cell block to be completed. This consisted of a central circular rotunda, called the Dome, with four wings extending north, south, east, and west in the shape of a cross. The cupola that topped the Dome was destroyed by fire during a riot in 1954 and never replaced.

Other buildings in the prison compound, which occupied around ten acres, housed industrial shops for various trades, such as blacksmithing, carpentry, tailoring, and rope manufacturing. Initially, it was surrounded by a twelve-foot-high cedar picket fence — the hulking limestone perimeter walls were completed only in 1845.

Beyond the walls, the site contained a series of stone quarries and a farm, which remained in operation until 1963.

The first six male inmates were ushered in on June 1, 1835, followed in early September by the first three women. In the early days, children as young as eight years old were also confined in this forbidding space.

Kingston Penitentiary in 1928, showing the northwest watch tower and north wall.

The first warden, Henry Smith, followed the penitentiary rules and regulations very closely. Take the requirement that there should be silence at all times, for example. As noted in *Kingston Penitentiary: The First Hundred and Fifty Years, 1835–1985*, Smith's sentences "ranged from six lashes of the cat-of-nine-tails for laughing, to bread and water diets 'for making a great noise in a cell by imitating the bark of a dog.'"

Children were singled out for particularly pitiless treatment: an eight-year-old boy, sentenced in 1845 to three years for pickpocketing, received the lash forty-seven times over a period of nine months for committing totally unacceptable offences such as giggling, whistling, and staring. For reasons unknown, a girl of twelve was flogged on six separate occasions.

And brutality, it seems, ran in the family. One of Smith's sons, employed in the penitentiary kitchen, was accused in a withering 1849 report of conducting inhumane practices, such as throwing hapless inmates into water barrels or using them as targets to improve his skills with a bow and arrow.

Given the tiny cells, physical toil, enforced silence, and brutal punishment at the hands of prison staff, it was not surprising that the incarcerated yearned to escape.

The first attempt took place in October 1836, when an inmate was discovered climbing over the wooden perimeter fence. He was rewarded with seven lashes and thrown into irons for months. In 1839, two women took advantage of the matron's trust — she had allowed one of them to lock herself, and others, into their cells. With keys in hand, the inmates simply unlocked the doors and walked away. A $100 reward was posted, and they were recaptured in Kingston the following day. After receiving a stern warning, the matron was permitted to keep her job.

In April 1904, *The Globe* newspaper revealed a particularly outrageous scheme to spring three "dangerous men" from custody. The trio, called the Welland Canal dynamiters, had languished in Kingston Pen for four years after an abortive attempt to blow up Lock 24 of the vital waterway linking Lake Ontario and Lake Erie. A sharp-eyed prison guard spotted a "bogus nun" slipping a package to one of the dynamiters during a visit, and money was later found hidden in the inmate's coat. The package had allegedly contained $1,000, to be used to bribe guards, but, perhaps unsurprisingly, most of the cash vanished, and the plot failed.

There were sporadic escapes over the years, including a breakout on horseback from the prison farm in 1914. But the numbers were small. In fact, according to figures provided by Canada's Penitentiary Museum, by 2013, when Canada's oldest maximum-security facility, notorious for its harsh conditions and for housing some of the country's most appalling and longest-serving criminals (child-killer Clifford Olson and serial killer Paul Bernardo spring to mind), closed for good, the final count of escapes from within the walled compound stood at thirty-four incidents, involving sixty-three individuals.

////////////////

Red Ryan's flamboyant getaway in 1923 was long flagged as the most spectacular of all. This record was shattered on August 17, 1947, however, when three "extremely dangerous" long-term prisoners broke free — amazingly, from the belly of the beast itself.

The undisputed leader of the threesome was twenty-five-year-old Ulysses Lauzon. In *What Happened to Mickey? The Life and Death of Donald "Mickey" McDonald, Public Enemy No. 1*, Peter McSherry quotes a fellow inmate of Lauzon's as saying "Lauzon exuded violence." Lauzon's previous claim to fame was that, after he and another bank robber escaped from the Waterloo County Jail in July 1945, the pair helped themselves to a staggering $351,000 from a Royal Bank of Canada branch in Bath, Ontario — this would be worth more than $6 million today. On September 13, 1945, *The Montreal Gazette* had described the heist as "the biggest bank holdup in the Dominion's history." Lauzon was nabbed in September of that year, sentenced to thirty-five years for three bank robberies and the jailbreak, and dispatched to Kingston Pen. Already a seasoned escape artist, he made it clear that he was not planning on a long stay.

Violent bank robber Ulysses Lauzon, the leader of a group of three men who escaped from the north wing of Kingston Penitentiary in August 1947.

Escapee Number Two was forty-year-old Donald John "Mickey" McDonald. (He changed his name from MacDonald to McDonald; both spellings are used.) McSherry notes that McDonald was called "dirty little Mickey from the Corner," which was the notorious intersection of Jarvis and Dundas in the Toronto neighbourhood referred to in the 1930s as Gangland. In 1942, McDonald was involved in a brawl at a Toronto hotel, during which an eighty-eight-year-old doorman was badly beaten. But he committed other far graver offences as well. At the time of the escape, he was serving a fifteen-year sentence for stealing a truckload of liquor worth $35,000 after a previous break from KP in 1943. And he had twice been tried for the brutal 1939 murder of flashy racketeer and bookie Jimmy Windsor in Windsor's Toronto home. Although weaknesses in the prosecution's case led to McDonald's acquittal, McSherry believes that he was, indeed, complicit in the killing.

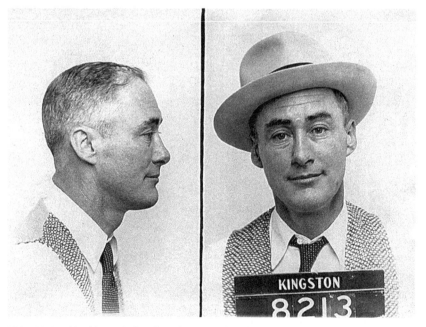

Mickey McDonald, robber and alleged murderer, one of the three "extremely dangerous" inmates who escaped from Kingston Penitentiary in 1947.

The last member of the escape team was Nicholas "Nick" Minelli, aged thirty-five, a professional thief from Ottawa who had started his criminal career while still a lad. This was his third term in Kingston. According to McSherry, Minelli, "bitter and resentful" at what he regarded as "a bum rap" for the violent kidnapping of an Ottawa taxi driver, was quite amenable to joining the others when invited.

Lauzon had discovered a flaw in the security of the penitentiary's seemingly impenetrable main building with its three-foot-thick walls and heavily barred windows — a trap door in the ceiling of a corridor on the top floor of the north wing. This led to an attic, where a small window gave access to the roof.

Fortuitously, the cells of all three men were located in the north cellblock.

Fellow inmates lavished the trio with hacksaws, a crowbar, lengths of rope made from mail bag strips, and sundry other useful items, and the plan

Nicholas "Nick" Minelli, jailed for a violent kidnapping, who escaped from Kingston Penitentiary with Lauzon and McDonald in August 1947.

was put into action just after midnight on August 18, 1947. As McSherry describes it, the three men placed life-like dummies in their beds with loaves of bread and real human hair for heads, stripped buck naked, greased their bodies with butter, and squeezed between the sawed-off bars of their cell gates. (Echoing this ploy five years later, members of the Boyd Gang slathered themselves with butter to slip between window bars and escape from death row at the Don Jail in Toronto.) The corridor, the unprotected trap door, and the attic were mere steps away. Within minutes, they had broken through the window and were on the roof.

Using one rope to drop down into the yard, the trio raced to the northeast corner of the prison carrying a grappling iron attached to a second rope, which they hooked onto a catwalk on a conveniently empty guard tower. After scaling the wall and sliding down the other side, they hot-wired a car belonging to a penitentiary guard who lived in the vicinity, and they were gone.

A huge police manhunt came up empty handed. A few days later Lauzon and McDonald popped up in Windsor, where they hit a bank for $50,000 before leaving the country.

The first of what were described as Canada's most hunted criminals was reeled in on May 18, 1948. A rookie cop in Oakland, California, found a man trying to break into a drugstore. The officer's suspicions were aroused when the burglar acted as though he'd been questioned before. A Federal Bureau of Investigation (FBI) fingerprint check revealed that John Carpenter of San Jose, California, was actually Nick Minelli, formerly of Kingston Penitentiary, Ontario. Before long, he was back in the Pen, where he remained until his discharge in 1959.

The "cocky, arrogant and boastful" Lauzon was much less fortunate. As reported in *The Kingston Whig-Standard* on July 29, 1948, under the banner headline "Gangsters Cut Down Lauzon in Mississippi: Bullet-pierced, Bludgeoned Body Discovered in Ditch," the local sheriff in nearby Pascagoula believed that Lauzon was probably slain by criminal associates who "thought he double crossed them in a divvy-up of spoils."

"What Happened to Mickey?" asks Peter McSherry, and, toward the end of his book, he provides the reader with several possible answers. He notes that according to veteran *Toronto Daily Star* reporter Gwyn "Jocko" Thomas, McDonald died with Lauzon in that Mississippi swamp near Pascagoula — like him, cut down for crossing local drug racketeers. Others in McDonald's circle believed that he had been murdered by hoods who didn't want to share the spoils after an armoured car robbery in Cincinnati, Ohio.

McSherry, however, accepts the story told to him by a man he calls Roy "Binky" Clarke, an acquaintance of both the McDonald family and most of those involved in the August 1947 escape from KP.

According to Clarke, Mickey met his end in the Hudson River in 1949. "He was in with this gang in New York.... One of the jobs he did for them was he got a Toronto engraver to go down to New York and cut counterfeit U.S. $10 and $20 plates for them."

Instead of keeping his mouth shut, Mickey boasted to the engraver about his connections with the mob. Instead of keeping his mouth shut, the engraver boasted about his accomplishments to random girls he met in a pub.

"A little stupid gossip. A little stupid bragging. Mickey died for that."

///////////////

Less than nine months after the trio's dead-of-the-night flight, another escape took place at Kingston Pen, this one in broad daylight; shockingly, two men would die.

John D. Kennedy, fifty-nine years old, was the KP messenger. His main duties included supervising prisoners who cleaned the office at the North (or front) Gate, moving official vehicles, chauffeuring senior staff on official business in and outside the grounds, and ferrying inmates and their officer escorts to hospital or the train station when necessary.

It was not part of Kennedy's usual duties to give inmates a ride, but that was what he was doing as he drove toward the North Gate at around 9:45 on the morning of April 26, 1948. In the car with him was Austin Craft, an inmate with special responsibilities and privileges — also known as a trusty. Craft, who hailed from the Maritimes, had served multiple sentences at KP, the latest being a ten-year stretch for holding up a bank with a cloth-covered car crank. Kennedy had befriended him and would often offer him a ride through the penitentiary grounds.

What Kennedy did not know was that another inmate, Howard Urquhart, serving a twenty-year sentence for his part in the murder of a Toronto furrier, was hiding in the trunk of the car. What Kennedy also didn't know was that Craft had obtained a gun, allegedly for a group of inmates planning an escape, but decided to keep the weapon for himself. He had either planted it in the car or hidden it near the gate.

Craft got out at the gate. After the vehicle passed into the passageway between the sturdy iron inner and outer barriers — which, for security reasons, were never open at the same time — Craft pulled out the weapon and, as reported in a *Globe and Mail* article on June 19, 1948, yelled, "This is it!"

A startled Kennedy jumped out of the car and ran to press the alarm.

He never reached it.

Craft's first shot pierced Kennedy's aorta, killing him, and he fired two more at the gatekeeper. He then threw open the outer barrier, while Urquhart scrambled out of the trunk and took the wheel. With Craft in the back seat, the car sped along King Street and out of town.

Around three hours later, a disciplined and grimly determined squad of armed penitentiary guards, Royal Canadian Mounted Police (RCMP), provincial, and city police, along with residents of the area, found the getaway car abandoned near Sydenham, around twenty-six kilometres northwest of Kingston. Two guards tracked the fugitives to a patch of dense brush at the side of the roadway.

In an April 1998 article for *The Kingston Whig-Standard* marking the fiftieth anniversary of John Kennedy's senseless murder, journalist Patrick Kennedy provided some of the details. "I had a .303 rifle at the ready because we didn't know if they were armed," said one of the guards who had captured the escapees. "They were huddled so close together I could've shot both with one shot, had they fired at us."

The escapees offered no resistance. Ironically, "Craft tossed the gun over his shoulder and shouted, 'Don't shoot; that would be murder and there are witnesses.'"

Kennedy has a special interest in the tragedy — John Kennedy was his uncle. In a personal interview, Patrick explained that his uncle's ties with the Kingston Penitentiary had been long and close. John's parents had lived for some years in an apartment located on the west wall of the prison, where six of their ten children, "including Johnny," were born. John's father, Michael, had himself been a messenger for a period of fifty-one years. His mother had a key to the front gate.

So, poignantly, John Kennedy was born, worked, and died in the Kingston Penitentiary.

The well-respected messenger was buried on April 29, 1948. A cortege of cars described as more than a mile long accompanied the hearse to St. Mary's Cemetery, where a crowd of around three hundred mourners was assembled.

Patrick Kennedy tells of the impact on his nuclear family of his uncle's shocking death. His father, Frank, shared a special bond with John, who was more of a surrogate father than an older brother. Tragically, Frank was driving past the penitentiary just after the escape when a guard recognized him and frantically called him over. Frank cradled

Well-respected Kingston Penitentiary messenger John D. Kennedy, who was shot and killed by inmate Austin Craft during a botched escape from the prison in April 1948.

his brother's limp body in his arms. The family believes that he never recovered from the trauma.

"I and I alone am responsible for the life that was taken," said Austin Craft at his preliminary hearing in June 1948. "I pulled the trigger, but I had no idea in the world of killing a man." As *The Globe and Mail* reported on June 19, 1948, he added: "I have sorrow for the life that was taken. He was my friend." He was "nervous," he said, and the gun "went off."

Craft was tried for murder in October 1948. After a two-day trial, he was found guilty with no recommendation for mercy. His sentence was death by hanging, as was the case for all those convicted of murder in Canada prior to the abolition of capital punishment in 1976.

The forty-nine-year-old man was executed just after midnight on January 24, 1949 — perhaps surprisingly, at the Frontenac County Gaol in Kingston. Many people question why the hanging did not take place at Kingston Pen, where the murder was committed. The simple answer is that Canadian penitentiaries are federal institutions; executions were the sole responsibility of local or provincial authorities.

As revealed in the *Globe* story of June 1948, twenty-one-year-old Howard Urquhart, Craft's fellow fugitive, told the court that Craft had approached him in the penitentiary garage on April 26 and asked "if I'd like to go home. I'm doing twenty years. I had nothing to lose. So I said yes." Urquhart was tried separately and sentenced to an additional seven years for escaping custody. In 2013, Urquhart's nephew-by-marriage told Patrick Kennedy that his uncle Howard had died of cancer in February of that year, at the ripe old age of eighty-seven.

///////////////

The coda to the saga of Kingston Penitentiary escapes would be written in 1999.

On May 6, thirty-two-year-old bank robber Tyrone Williams "Ty" Conn, after voicing his despair at his failure to be granted a transfer to a medium-security prison, left a note on his calendar ("FISHING TRIP '99") and a dummy in his cell before using a ladder and a grappling hook he had fashioned in the prison canvas shop to go over the wall — the first successful escape since 1958. At the time, he was serving a staggering forty-seven years for a series of bank robberies and prison escapes.

Born in 1967 to a sixteen-year-old mother and a slightly older father and given up by both (although he did reestablish close contact with his mother in later years), Ty Conn, born Ernest Bruce Hayes, was placed for adoption at the age of three. He was taken in by a couple from Belleville, Ontario. His adoptive mother became increasingly unstable, and the boy was serially abused. By the age of eleven, he was again surrendered into care. For years, he rattled around, shunted from foster homes to group homes to youth detention centres.

Between the ages of thirteen and thirty-two, Conn was described as having been "legally at large"— that is, neither in prison nor on the lam — for just sixty-nine days.

Conn expressed an enduring admiration for Edwin Alonzo Boyd, who was famous not only for robbing banks but for escaping twice from Toronto's forbidding Don Jail. As revealed in a *Globe and Mail* special in May 1999, Conn had commented in a 1997 letter to Brian Vallée, who wrote a book about Boyd's exploits: "Boyd's attitude of not wanting to hurt anyone during his career has stuck with me to this day, and fortunately in 13 years of robbing places I have never once hurt or shot at anyone. That's why I choose to believe Mr. Boyd's style had a good effect on me."

On May 20, 1999, alone in a squalid basement apartment in Toronto surrounded by a cordon of armed police, Conn shot himself, apparently while trying to negotiate a surrender over the phone with CBC producer-turned-friend Theresa Burke.

In an interesting parallel with Ernest Hemingway and his reportage of the Red Ryan escape, another media personality and novelist turned his hand to documenting the case of Ty Conn. With fellow journalist Burke, Linden MacIntyre wrote a searing exposé, entitled *Who Killed Ty Conn*, first published in 2000.

Their summing up? Ty Conn was bright and articulate, with "a capacity for deep reflection that is rare." But his life, sadly, driven by maltreatment and rejection, rapidly descended into a spiral of anti-social and criminal behaviour. Instead of breaking that vicious cycle and rehabilitating him, the law enforcement and incarceration he was subjected to failed him. Miserably.

Robert Clark, who spent thirty years in the Canadian prison service, devotes a whole chapter to Conn in his memoir *Down Inside*. Clark claims adamantly that the decision taken in 1999 by KP authorities, including himself as a senior manager, not to recommend Conn for transfer to a lower-security institution was the correct one. In spite of a stellar reputation among his fellow inmates, Conn had been a jailhouse informant for years. According to the powers that be, Conn's aims were hardly altruistic: he was suspected of seeking a transfer out of maximum-security Kingston to facilitate yet another escape.

This decision was supported by a Correctional Service Canada investigation after Conn's death, which, as Clark notes, concluded that he was "appropriately placed at Kingston Penitentiary."

Was Conn being "morally and socially responsible" in 1998, when he risked the vengeance of fellow inmates by giving advance warning to prison authorities about a mass breakout, as MacIntyre and Burke suggest, or merely cynically gaming the system?

We shall never know.

What remains is a statistic. At number sixty-three, Ty Conn's was the last successful escape from KP, if you can call successful an abortive and hopeless endeavour that ended with a self-inflicted death.

///////////////

When it came to escapes, then, Fortress Kingston was largely successful in tamping down its tally.

In other respects, however, the prison received a failing grade. Penal studies repeatedly underscore the dangers of a transient prison population, overcrowding, and maximum security, along with uncontrolled access to alcohol and drugs. On multiple occasions, these factors combined to make KP a grim crucible of violence, suicide, and death during the 178 years it served as Canada's most notorious carceral institution.

And a frenzied four-day orgy of destruction in April 1971 would have a deleterious knock-on effect at another bleak correctional facility — Millhaven Institution, located at Bath, just twenty-five kilometres west of Kingston.

4

High Flyer

The Ups and Downs of "Flying Bandit" Kenneth Leishman

AT 2:40 ON THE AFTERNOON OF DECEMBER 17, 1957, POSING AS A businessman from Buffalo, William Kenneth Leishman strode into the Toronto Dominion Bank at the corner of Yonge and Albert Streets in downtown Toronto and asked to see A.J. Lunn, the manager.

The Ottawa Citizen of July 18, 1958, gave the full scoop on what happened next.

Once comfortably seated in Lunn's office with the door shut, Leishman produced a .22 Luger, saying, "Mr. Lunn, as you obviously realize, this is a holdup."

Leishman's ask was $10,000. Lunn made out a counter cheque for that amount, initialled it, and accompanied Leishman to the teller's cage to get it cashed. Duped by Leishman's warm smile and friendly conversation into believing that the two men were old pals, the teller handed Leishman the cash in large bills.

"Come on, Mr. Lunn," said Leishman to the traumatized manager, "I'll buy you a cup of coffee."

The two left the building together. When they parted ways, Lunn rushed back to the bank to report the robbery. Leishman drove his rental car back to Toronto's Malton (now Pearson) Airport and flew home to his family in Winnipeg.

Born in rural Manitoba in June 1931, during the dark days of the Depression, Kenneth Leishman had a tumultuous early life. When he was seven his parents separated, leaving his mother to raise three children alone. She managed to find live-in domestic work for a widowed farmer, but he hated the boy and subjected him to physical abuse. Faced with an ultimatum from her employer, Leishman's mother reluctantly sent her son away.

After being shuttled from relatives to friends to foster homes, Leishman eventually found some stability as a fourteen-year-old, working on his grandparents' farm, and at age sixteen he reconnected with his father.

In February 1950, Leishman married Elva Shields, and the couple settled in Winnipeg. Their first few months of married life were marked by Leishman's first foray into crime. To furnish their new apartment he stole a radio, a Westinghouse fridge and range, and an assortment of household goods from Genser's Furniture, for a total value of around $1,000. These larcenous activities earned him a nine-months' jail sentence, reduced to four months for good behaviour.

On his release from jail, Leishman turned to a passion that he would pursue for the rest of his days: flying. He took lessons and before long had purchased his own plane, which he flew into rural areas for both work and pleasure.

After scrolling through a series of short-term positions between 1950 and 1956, Leishman finally found a lucrative sales job with a cookware company. In late 1957, however, the business folded, leaving him out of work just before Christmas. With a wife and four children to support and his penchant for the finer things in life — snazzy clothing, a solid home in Winnipeg, a Cadillac, and even his own three-seater airplane — he was living way beyond his means. And creditors were snapping at his heels.

He had to take swift action to extricate himself from the mess. And the only solution, as he saw it, was to fly to Toronto and rob a bank.

Why Toronto? As per *The Ottawa Citizen* in July 1958, Leishman explained it thus: "Out west, people have lots of money but it's tied up in land and farm machinery.... But out east they work with cash." And logically, the best place to find this ready money would be in a bank.

So, on December 16, 1957, Leishman packed a bag, kissed his wife and kids goodbye, and boarded a plane bound for Toronto — the very image of a successful salesman on a business trip. On arrival, he rented a car and drove into the city, where he checked into the ritzy Park Plaza Hotel. After a good night's sleep, he was ready to face the day. In the morning, he did some shopping; in the afternoon, he hit the TD Bank in downtown Toronto.

Back in Winnipeg with $10,000 burning a hole in his pocket (roughly equivalent to $109,000 today), he bought his wife a mink stole and splurged on Christmas gifts for the kids.

Leishman had been toying with the idea of opening a luxurious fly-in fishing lodge in northern Manitoba for the titillation of rich Americans. In March 1958, he returned to Toronto with a view to raking in some working capital. One source suggests that he was looking for $25,000 to cover initial costs; according to another, he was angling for $40,000.

Brimming with confidence, Leishman strode into the Canadian Imperial Bank of Commerce at the congested corner of Yonge and Bloor Streets. His first bank job had been a rip-roaring success, with police still perplexed as to the identity of the perpetrator of one of the most audacious robberies on record. The second would surely be just as easy.

This time, however, the bank manager did not take kindly to the gun pointed at his chest; instead, he yelled for his staff to sound the alarm. A panicked Leishman fled down Yonge Street. He did not get far. He either tripped or was tripped, and he found himself looking into the barrel of a police revolver.

After his arrest, Leishman made the mistake of sharing the details of his first, as yet unsolved, holdup with a fellow detainee, who turned out to be a police informer. When the story hit the headlines, the public was entranced by the exploits of the dapper, dignified, smooth-talking "perfect gentleman," who commuted to Toronto to rob banks.

Dubbed the "Flying Bandit," Leishman pleaded guilty to the two robberies and was sentenced in April 1958 to twelve years for one count of armed robbery and one count of attempted armed robbery, to be served at the Stony Mountain Penitentiary just outside Winnipeg. Once again, he did not serve the full sentence. Described as a model prisoner, he was paroled after just three and a half years.

Leishman's life of crime seemed to be well and truly over. For four years he toed the line, working mainly as a door-to-door salesman. But by 1966, with seven children now in the family, he felt a pressing need to explore other sources of revenue.

///////////////////

"BULLION SHIPMENT STOLEN AT WINNIPEG," screamed the headlines in Regina's *Leader-Post* on March 2, 1966. The article went on to explain that two men in stolen Air Canada coveralls "carried a stolen Air Canada order form and got away in a truck stolen from the same airline." What they whisked away from Winnipeg International Airport was a shipment of twelve boxes of gold, valued at a staggering $383,497 (that would be around $3.5 million today), newly arrived from Red Lake aboard a Transair DC-3 and bound for the Royal Canadian Mint in Ottawa.

"This wasn't done by the same guys who knock over the corner drug store," said a Transair official plaintively.

In fact, the mastermind behind this daring escapade was none other than Ken Leishman, aided and abetted by Winnipeg lawyer Harry Backlin. The remaining three gang members, so-called bar buddies of Leishman's, contributed to the heist by driving the stolen truck and the getaway vehicle.

The robbery was meticulously researched and executed, but, similar to other Leishman ventures, it soon unravelled. Police found telltale fingerprints in the stolen vehicle and most of the gold buried in Backlin's backyard. By March 16, all five offenders were in custody.

After the preliminary hearing in May 1966, during which the Crown came down hard on Leishman and his accomplices, Leishman was committed to stand trial on charges of theft and conspiracy. Denied bail, he was sent to Headingley Gaol (now called Headingley Correctional Centre), a provincial institution for short-term offenders on the north bank of the Assiniboine River to the west of Winnipeg. Inmates included those awaiting trial, appeal, or transfer to another institution.

Leishman spent the summer sequestered with some twenty other men in Headingley's foul remand cage. Anticipating a lengthy sentence for the gold heist in addition to the remainder of the time he would now have to serve for the bank holdups, Leishman's driving purpose became to find a way out.

This was no easy task. Three sets of steel bars stood between him and the great outdoors: the first set formed the perimeter of the remand cage, the second separated the prisoners' section from the administration area, and the third blocked off the front door.

At around seven o'clock on the evening of Thursday, September 1, the lone guard in charge of the remand cage was trussed up and gagged after being tricked into entering the enclosure to check on a supposedly sick inmate. Within fifteen minutes, all eleven guards at the facility had been overpowered and locked up. One of them was forced to open the wall safe in the office, giving the escapees access to guns and ammo. The prisoners also located their street clothes, neatly stored and labelled in a basement storeroom.

Although many of the cell doors had been flung open, only ten of the 350-odd inmates seized the opportunity to flee. Still, the escape touched off one of the biggest manhunts in Manitoba history. Police set up roadblocks, and airports and border crossings were strictly monitored.

Six of the jailbreakers were speedily recaptured. The remaining four, who had scrambled into a Chevy sedan owned by a guard, got clean away.

And what a motley bunch they were!

Ken Leishman, who had instigated the getaway, was an armed bank robber and gold thief. His companions were Joseph William Dale, armed robber and rapist; George Leclerc, a Montreal conman charged with false pretenses and theft; and Barry Kay Duke, who had been acquitted of killing his girlfriend on grounds of insanity. Duke was being kept under heavy sedation at Headingley until such time as the authorities could work out what to do with him. Leishman was thirty-four at the time; the others were all in their twenties.

Leishman's plan was to steal a plane and head down south, across the United States border. After an abortive attempt to make off with an aircraft from the nearby air base in Warren, the four fugitives dumped the car and proceeded on foot. Hours later, they came across a farmhouse, empty of occupants but with clothes in a closet, cash hidden in a Bible, and a freezer full of food to help them along the way.

At around 2:00 a.m. on Saturday, September 3, the footsore foursome came across a young couple kissing and cuddling in the back seat of a brand-new Chevy Malibu. After hijacking the car and kidnapping its occupants at gunpoint, the escapees headed for an airport on the outskirts of Steinbach, to the southeast of Winnipeg.

Their luck was in. Parked in a hanger was a Mooney Mark 21, a single engine aircraft that could accommodate the pilot and up to three passengers. The fact that the keys were missing was not a problem. They hastily hot-wired the plane, and by 8:00 a.m., they were in the air, heading across the border, while their erstwhile captives sped into town to alert the Royal Canadian Mounted Police (RCMP).

"Was I worried? No! [Leishman] was very nice," Heather Jackson said after the event, as per a lengthy *Winnipeg Sun* article in August 2003. "They were all very nice. We certainly had nothing to worry about."

The escapees were unable to refuel at Tyler, Minnesota, or Okoboji, Iowa. They finally managed to gas up at Springfield, Iowa. By then, Leishman had decided to look up a contact in Gary, Indiana, and he landed the plane in a cornfield some fifteen miles to the southeast of the city.

"Didn't hurt the field a bit," said farmer Russ Shook laconically.

By six o'clock that evening, the fugitives had arrived in rough-and-ready Gary, where their luck ran out. The owner of a bar overheard four beer-swilling customers chatting about stealing a plane. After learning about the downed aircraft on the evening news, he called the police. By the time a contingent of sixty cops arrived, the four Canadians had retired to rooms rented in the Baltimore Hotel next door to the bar.

Leishman and Duke were captured without incident. Leclerc and Dale, however, traded bullets with police as they dashed across the rooftops to avoid capture. Leclerc was shot in the wrist and Dale, too, was wounded before both were taken into custody.

"We're fellows guilty of wanting our freedom, nothing more," Leishman protested during his brief incarceration at the Lake County Jail, Indiana. They were certainly not a "bunch of mad dog killers," he told a reporter from *The Brandon Sun* on September 6, 1966, and he denied that they were "armed in any manner to combat a police force."

The police were unconvinced. They claimed that they had found a small arsenal of guns and knives in the aircraft and noted that all the fugitives were carrying automatic pistols.

On Friday, September 9, the four escapees and an RCMP escort boarded an otherwise empty Air Canada flight bound for Winnipeg.

The infuriated Manitoban authorities threw the book at Leishman. His charges included escaping from jail with violence, car theft, housebreaking, stealing food, clothing, and money, unlawfully confining the young couple whose car they had hijacked, and theft of an airplane valued at $11,000.

Despite being guarded around the clock in a separate section at Winnipeg's bleak eighty-five-year-old Vaughan Street Jail, Leishman managed to escape yet again. On the evening of October 30, 1966, armed with a sawed-off steel pipe, he overpowered three guards, tied them up, and grabbed their keys. After unlocking the outer door to reach the exercise yard, he scaled the perimeter fence and fled.

At 7:30 p.m., an emergency bulletin announced, to the delight of many Winnipeggers and the disquiet of others, that the irrepressible Flying Bandit had again flown the coop.

This time, however, his taste of freedom was just that — a taste.

Within four hours he was spotted in a phone booth a few kilometres from the jail. Exhausted and with an injured hand and bleeding feet, he meekly held out his wrists to be handcuffed by the two cops who had nabbed him.

As reported in the 2003 *Winnipeg Sun* article, his comment to his captors was "I'm not a violent man."

"Flying Bandit" Kenneth Leishman and an RCMP escort returning to Winnipeg on September 9, 1966, following Leishman's extradition from the United States.

In court on November 1, Leishman pleaded guilty to all charges. He was sentenced to five years for breaking out of Headingley and two for the Vaughan Street escape, to be added to the time remaining on his bank robbery sentence. His sentence for the gold heist could have been catastrophic: anything from ten years to life. Amazingly, the judge decided on a lenient term of eight years, to run concurrently with the others.

Leishman escaped from prison one last time — legally, as the result of an administrative snafu. With confusion over the exact length of his various overlapping sentences, some running consecutively and others concurrently, and a morass of convoluted parole regulations, Ken convinced the parole board in early 1974 that he had actually served his full sentence, and then some.

The upshot was that on May 3, 1974, Kenneth Leishman walked out of Stony Mountain Institution where he had served most of his time — a free man at last.

"Don't ask us how it works," was *The Globe and Mail*'s caustic summing-up on May 8, 1974. "The public will be left too exhausted for a while to ask why the National Parole Board and the Canadian Penitentiary Service want to make things so complicated."

In 1975, Leishman and his family moved to Red Lake, 430 kilometres northwest of Thunder Bay — coincidentally, the place where that famous hijacked consignment of gold bullion had originated. He became the proprietor of a clothing store and, in an exceptionally ironic twist, president of the chamber of commerce. He even came close to being elected reeve.

The Edmonton Journal of March 11, 1978, quoted an admiring local businessman as saying, "He's just the kind of guy we need, a real go-getter."

///////////////

In 1981, Heather Robertson authored the appropriately titled *The Flying Bandit*, a chronicle of the topsy-turvy life of William Kenneth Leishman. In an interview at the time, she presented a nuanced assessment of the man's strengths and weaknesses, summing him up as "a kind of everyman," but one who had "lost touch with the line between fantasy and reality." She noted his Jekyll-and-Hyde nature: a charming and likeable gentleman on the one hand, a daring, sharp-eyed, and meticulous schemer on the other. Unfortunately for him, "he was a bit of a klutz, a comic-hero. Not someone you would want to emulate. He was constantly blowing it. He'd pull off the perfect crime and then open his mouth." And he was incredibly unlucky to boot.

Some, though, have labelled Leishman "Dillingeresque," a reference to U.S. Depression–era gang leader and prolific bank robber John Dillinger, who went to prison multiple times and escaped twice. Like Leishman, Dillinger's first bank robbery netted $10,000; in toto his robberies brought in more than $300,000. Like Leishman, Dillinger basked in the public eye and he, too, was described by the media as being a Robin Hood–type figure, cheered on by regular folks for rebelling against authority and robbing the rich.

But there were significant differences. Dillinger was a violent criminal accused (although not convicted) of murder. He died in a hail of bullets in Chicago during an exchange of gunfire with police.

Leishman certainly carried weapons and was not averse to using guns as a threat — and he struck prison guards with a steel pipe during his escape from Winnipeg's Vaughan Street Jail — but he was not intrinsically violent. And his end, although newsworthy, could not have been more different from Dillinger's.

On December 14, 1979, Leishman carried out a mercy flight to a remote First Nations reserve in northern Ontario to ferry a severely injured woman and her nurse to hospital in Thunder Bay. Contact was lost with his small, twin-engine plane at around 8:25 p.m., just five minutes before it was due to land in Thunder Bay. Although it was presumed that the plane had crashed, extensive searches carried out at the time proved fruitless. It was not until May 1980 that a Canadian Forces rescue team in a helicopter spotted the wreckage strewn about in a hilly, forested area around forty kilometres north of the city.

All that remained of the plane's occupants were shreds of clothing and fragments of bone, which were sent to the Centre of Forensic Sciences in Toronto for analysis. The remains of the two women were positively identified; however, as noted in *The Leader-Post* on September 27, 1980, the coroner stated that "no positive identification on Leishman has been made." With no absolute proof of identity, Leishman was regarded as still officially alive. But experts were in agreement that nobody could have escaped the crash and that his body had probably been dragged away by wild animals.

Some wondered at the time, and have speculated since, whether Leishman was indeed dead — especially in light of the fact that a sizable chunk of one of the gold bars stolen in the 1966 heist was never recovered. As reported in *The Globe and Mail* two days after Leishman's inquest on December 16, 1980, Leishman's son, Wade, had vigorously denied the rumours. "He had no life insurance and no motive," he told the inquest. "I believe my father died on Dec. 14 [1979]."

On December 16, 1980, one year and two days after his plane plummeted into the rugged northern Ontario hinterland, William Kenneth Leishman was declared legally deceased.

But the legend and the mystery of the Flying Bandit live on.

5

Maximum Security

A Record-Setting Breakout from a Canadian Federal Prison

KINGSTON PENITENTIARY, APRIL 14, 1971.

"It was on a Wednesday around 10 p.m. when the repressive and dehumanizing conditions inside the 140-year-old cauldron finally reached the point where the lid blew off.... A colossal beehive overturned and overrun by prisoners running amok. Intoxicated with rage and pent-up frustration, they vented their fury with inhuman strength," wrote habitual criminal and serial escapee Roger Caron in his prison memoir *Go-Boy! This Is the True Story of Life Behind Bars*. To his misfortune, Caron was in the Pen at the time awaiting the outcome of an appeal.

The bloody four-day riot that followed saw six guards taken hostage, fourteen "undesirables" (sex offenders and informants) tortured and two of them murdered, and large sections of the main cellblock utterly destroyed.

After the dust and considerable debris had settled, an official inquiry chaired by Justice J.W. Swackhamer drilled down to the roots of the insurrection. These included "the aged physical facilities, overcrowding, the shortage of professional staff," and much too much time spent in cells, as well as a total breakdown in communication between inmates and prison officials.

Something noted in the report and emphasized by the news media of the day: Kingston inmates were spooked by the mere thought of ending up in the newly built Millhaven Institution with, to quote *The Toronto Daily Star* of April 20, 1971, its "push-button gadgetry, snoop microphones, closed-circuit surveillance TV and one-way glass."

The Canadian government had announced in 1964 that an $18-million state-of-the-art prison complex was to be built some twenty kilometres to the west of Kingston to replace antiquated and chronically overcrowded Fortress Kingston — although, as it turned out, KP would close only in 2013. Starting in the 1940s, a new system of classifying prisons based upon security level had been introduced. Millhaven, like Kingston, would be designated as maximum security.

Millhaven became the latest in a series of federal penal institutions to be built in the Greater Kingston area. In fact, as pointed out on the Canadian Penitentiary Museum website, at one time or another there were an astonishing ten minimum-, medium-, and maximum-security penitentiaries operating in or around Kingston, including Bath Institution, Joyceville Institution, and Collins Bay Institution, all classified as medium-security, and the multilevel Prison for Women.

Two of the main reasons given for the concentration of correctional facilities in this area are that Ontario is the most densely populated region in Canada with correspondingly higher crime rates and that Kingston is sandwiched between the major centres of Toronto and Montreal, with Ottawa fairly close by. Additionally, both the know-how required to operate prisons of all types and the inmate labour force often corralled for new builds were already in place. All of these factors made it more cost-effective to build new institutions where older ones already existed.

Correctional Service Canada describes Millhaven on its website as being "based on a radial design model where offender accommodations are direct observation living units (read: cell blocks) radiating off a central control post." Catherine Fogarty, in *Murder on the Inside: The True Story of the Deadly Riot at Kingston Penitentiary*, paints it in a more sinister light as "an octopus, low to the ground with tentacles forming a network of escape-proof cells."

On the morning of the riot in April 1971, the first twelve inmates had been transferred from Kingston to Millhaven. With the new prison still under construction and not yet fully staffed, the plan was to fill the place gradually, moving across a total of forty inmates per month. That plan went out the window as, with their KP quarters in ruins after the riot, close to four hundred inmates were unceremoniously bused to dreaded Millhaven. Roger Caron was one of the transferees. He grimly describes the gauntlet of baton-wielding guards that greeted them, hell-bent on wreaking vengeance on the rioters: "With our hands and feet shackled we could only shuffle down the long hallway as the clubs rained down upon us, crunching through bone and muscle."

Hardly an auspicious beginning for the facility, and one that laid the foundation for an astounding nineteen major incidents in the first six years of its existence.

In October 1971, the federal commissioner of penitentiaries announced that a shiny new feature — 4,200 feet of barbed wire (that's nearly 1,300 metres) — would be installed around the penitentiary to prevent convicts from scaling the parallel lines of fourteen-foot-high heavy gauge steel chain-link perimeter fencing. This would add another measure to the current security setup, which included the two fences, three watch towers equipped with searchlights and armed guards, and a vehicle patrol outside the prison.

This attempt to buff up security did nothing to avert the first of those nineteen major incidents: an escape in December 1971 from the "virtually escape-proof" prison, or what *The Ottawa Citizen* in July 1972 sarcastically called the "foolproof pen."

The man who scored the historic first was Thomas William McCauley, serving twenty-five years for a mixed bag of serious crimes: attempted

A nighttime view of Millhaven Institution taken round 1975, showing the fence line and perimeter lighting.

murder, armed robbery, break and enter, escaping custody, forgery, and uttering or knowingly using a falsified document. McCauley, thirty-four years old and heavily tattooed on both hands and forearms, was described by prison authorities as an "extremely dangerous" individual who "should be approached with extreme caution."

Prison officials were not quite sure *when* he escaped, although they did know *how*. He simply forced a lock in the print shop and then cut through a gate in the perimeter fence. For his convenience, barbed wire had not yet been installed at this gate, as it was being used by the construction workers putting finishing touches to the prison. McCauley discarded a white sheet near the fence. It had evidently served him as camouflage when crossing the snow-covered yard.

Initial reports suggested that he was probably headed for Montreal. However, he was located on December 4 by an Ontario Provincial Police (OPP) officer and his tracking dog in a bushy area eight kilometres west of the prison. Although he had spent two days in below-freezing temperatures, McCauley was seemingly not too much worse for wear.

McCauley's initial escape turned out to be merely the dress rehearsal for a much splashier show seven months later.

At around 9:00 p.m. on Monday, July 10, 1972, over a hundred men were milling about in the compound, either watching or participating in a ball game. Despite the presence of guards in each of the three watch towers, a group of inmates succeeded in cutting their way through the fencing after the game. The guards were unaware that anything was amiss, but, around twenty-five minutes later, a head count revealed that at least three men were absent. In short order, that number was upped to fourteen. A hasty search along the wire was carried out and a telltale gaping hole discovered.

As reported in *The Globe and Mail* on July 12, 1972, there was inadequate lighting along this section of the fence. Millhaven director Donald Clark blamed the breakout on a "vulnerable spot." He scoffed at claims that the prison was escape-proof. "Anyone thinking that, considering the fact that we have a fence instead of a wall, would have to be terribly naive," he said.

What about all the heavy barbed wire recently installed around the perimeter? As *The Kingston Whig-Standard* noted on July 11, 1972, the laconic response from a prison official was "I assume they took it in their stride."

The breakout was, and still is, the largest ever recorded from a federal institution in Canada.

The escapees, all in their twenties or thirties, had chalked up quite an impressive tally of crimes: three were serving time for murder or manslaughter, nine for robbery, and two for break and enter. And the majority had been charged with more than one offence. Interestingly, there were no sex offences on the list, no drug offences, and no direct links to organized crime.

Roads around the area were immediately cordoned off by penitentiary guards and police officers armed with shotguns and high-powered rifles, and tracker dogs were brought in.

Local authority and history buff Steven E. Silver recalls the "absolute climate of fear" that blanketed the area in the summer of 1972. You couldn't go anywhere without running into a roadblock. Everybody was on edge. People carried guns.

That summer, a teenaged Silver and his family were camping in a nearby park. His father, Ernest, a guard at medium-security Collins Bay in Kingston, assured his family that the escapees were not in the area but still insisted on precautions — no one was to leave the campsite after dark, for example. Also, he issued a stern warning to his son: "You see one of them, you don't approach them. You come and get me right away."

Four of the escapees had little more than a tantalizing glimpse of the outside before being whisked back in again. All of them were caught on the evening of July 11, within an eight-to-ten-kilometre radius of the prison.

Fugitive Number Five was also apprehended on July 11, after running afoul of brothers William and Raymond Newbury. Late that evening, William spotted a man behaving erratically near their farmhouse, a short distance to the west of the prison. The brothers set out in their truck to investigate.

As Raymond later told the press, the man, whom he described as having long hair that stood out like the mane of a horse, ran like hell when he saw them.

The two farmers found him cowering in a grassy ditch and hauled him out. Within minutes, an OPP cruiser came by and relieved the brothers of their charge. He turned out to be Gaston Lambert, twenty-two, serving fifteen years for several offences, including armed robbery.

As sidenotes to the main events, John Singleton, an escapee from nearby Collins Bay, was captured on July 12 on the Canadian National Railway tracks to the north of Millhaven. He had strolled away from a work gang on July 11, totally oblivious of the mass breakout. And the only fatality came in an accident when correctional officer Wallace Lloyd was killed after losing control of his vehicle on his way home from a shift at a roadblock.

On July 13, two young friends on a farm just outside Napanee made a dramatic discovery: a stranger hiding in the barn. When the boys sprinted back to the farmhouse, the man chased after them and pushed his way into the house. He was met by Theresa Miller, at home with seven children. Miller had no difficulty in reaching the conclusion that their uninvited "guest" — shoeless, bedraggled, and wearing prison garb — was one of the Millhaven escapees.

She did what any sensible mom might do when confronted by a seemingly "timid" but potentially dangerous intruder — she fed him.

"I made him four bologna sandwiches and gave him a big piece of lemon meringue pie that I pulled from the oven," the then eighty-six-year-old Miller reminisced in an exclusive interview with *The Kingston Whig-Standard* in July 2022.

She also calmly showed him newspaper reports about the fugitives who had already been recaptured (five) and discussed his chances of getting away (zero). And, while he munched on his sandwiches and pie, she called the cops. The man, thirty-two-year-old Richard "Buddy" Smith, sentenced to twelve years on seven counts of armed robbery, took the phone from her to identify himself and assure the police that he meant no harm to the family. He then used the absent Mr. Miller's shaving kit to spruce himself up. He was playing ball with the kids when officers arrived to cart him away.

By July 13, Canadian forces had arrived to swell the ranks. As reported in the press, three hundred military personnel, two hundred OPP officers, fifty guards, seven dogs, four aircraft and two boats were now involved in the search.

Amid the mounting anxiety, Donald Parkinson, a care-home orderly from Odessa, was abducted near his house in the early morning hours of July 16. His lone assailant, whom he described as standing five feet ten inches tall and wearing a grey shirt and pants, forced him at knifepoint to drive to Montreal.

"I asked him if he wanted to take the truck and leave me behind because I was concerned about that knife sticking in my ribs," *The Kingston-Whig Standard* reported on July 18, 1972. His abductor refused. Before they reached their destination, the man ordered Parkinson to stop the truck and strip off his uniform. After changing into Parkinson's clothing, the man ran away.

Parkinson caused quite a stir when he walked into a nearby motel clad only in his underwear. After spending several hours with the Montreal police, he was free to make his way home, in clothes supplied by the Salvation Army.

"It was an experience I'd just as soon forget," said Parkinson. "So as soon as I got home, I had a couple of stiff belts of rye."

As described in the same issue of the paper, however, some folks were totally unfazed by the military and police units combing the area. A woman in the little hamlet of Conway said: "None of us is nervous. My husband is out in the fields raking hay this morning and one of my boys is out in the barn." The boy, all of seven years old, wasn't afraid "because he has a pitchfork." The rest of her kids thought "it's just too exciting."

William Yardley, twenty-four years old and serving twelve years for robbery, was recaptured on July 17 in what *The Kingston Whig-Standard* described that day as "a dramatic, concentrated manhunt by provincial police and army troops." The search began when a burglary was reported by Bernice Milligan, a widow living in a small house near the Bath marina. Police scrambled to the scene and found that someone had broken in through a small window at the back of the dwelling. After making a careful inventory of her pantry, Milligan declared that the thief had made off with several cans of soup and a can of beans. The intruder had the presence of mind to grab a can opener, too, but dropped it during his hasty retreat.

With the help of soldiers, tracker dogs, and a helicopter, the police pursued Yardley for nine hours before pinning him down in dense bush to the south of Millhaven. Still in prison gear, his hair long and shaggy and his face haggard, Yardley put up no resistance when he was finally cornered.

In a 2022 *Kingstonist* interview entitled "Officer Recalls the Summer of '72 Millhaven Escape," published exactly fifty years after the dramatic prison break, retired OPP officer P.J. McCaffrey described his role in the largest manhunt in Canadian history. He was serving as a motorcycle cop when he received a late-night call on July 10 from his commander. "I go in there with my bloody bike uniform on ... leathers and all," he told interviewer Michelle Dorey Forestell, "and the next thing I know, I'm going through swamps. Holy ... this isn't fun at all."

McCaffrey soon abandoned his bike for a police cruiser, working with dog handlers and their animals. According to McCaffrey, his team travelled "almost 10,000 miles" across Ontario within the space of two months. They also spent hours trudging through swamps and woodlands in the crushing July heat.

At four o'clock one morning, "this guy pulls in … Ray Carson with [his dog] Cloud. He says, 'I'm gonna need somebody with me.' … They said, 'You go with them' … I grabbed the shotgun … I got a car and I went with Ray because he was from North Bay and didn't know the area."

Cloud's full name was Cloud II. At the time, the powerful German Shepherd, the second of three Clouds trained by Constable (later Staff Sergeant) Carson, was on the brink of an illustrious career in the OPP's canine unit.

The incident McCaffrey remembers most vividly took place just outside Napanee.

On the night of July 17, after around forty hours without sleep, the two men and their dog pulled up at a roadblock near Lake Ontario to take a nap. By then, the officers had ditched their uniforms in favour of cooler and more comfortable jeans, boots, and OPP shirts. They had not rested for long before a telephone tip came in about a stranger who had terrified a local woman by banging on her door before fleeing along the railway tracks.

"I knew the area, so we went [and] parked the car along the tracks," explained McCaffrey. "I grab the two-way radio — like holy jeez that sucker weighed about 15 pounds — so I won't take the shotgun this time; it's likely just a hobo wandering the tracks."

It was no hobo.

As they scrambled along the rails, Cloud started pulling at the long tracking lead. He made for a tangle of shrubs and growled fiercely.

And there, cowering beneath a bush, was Donald Oag.

Twenty-two-year-old Oag, believed to have masterminded the escape with Thomas McCauley, had been serving time at Kingston Pen in April 1971. After the riot, Oag had been implicated with his brother James in the murder of Bertrand Henry Robert, one of the so-called undesirables. Both brothers had pleaded guilty to the lesser charge of manslaughter. James had also ended up in Millhaven but had not taken part in the escape.

"We would have missed him — but Cloud didn't miss him," smiled McCaffrey.

While Carson restrained Cloud, McCaffrey held his gun against Oag's ear. "You move and I'll blow your … head off," he said, his expletive tactfully omitted in the *Kingstonist* article. To which the man responded, "Don't let the dog bite me."

As Steven Silver puts it: "Cons in general were terrified of the dogs. More afraid than of the guy with the rifle."

Anecdotally, all Oag had on him when he was recaptured was a small green apple. McCaffrey disputes this, saying that he relieved the man of a large pair of pliers.

Another early morning telephone tip on the same day, this one anonymous, led police to the whereabouts of the tenth member of the Millhaven 14. Twenty-five-year-old armed robber Rudolph Nuss, also regarded as extremely dangerous, had made a beeline for his parents' house in Niagara-on-the-Lake. He was seized uneventfully at the family home by a combined force of OPP and Niagara Regional Police.

By July 20, 1972, with four men still at large — Thomas McCauley, Gerald Larocque, Charles Boomer, and Sreto Dzambas — the hunt was flagging. Temperatures in excess of twenty-seven degrees, extreme humidity, and clouds of mosquitoes played havoc with the tempers of the searchers. The next day, police roadblocks were discontinued and military personnel were cut. And two weeks after the prison break, the army was withdrawn from Millhaven.

Oag's co-conspirator, Thomas McCauley, would prove to be slippery. A couple of days after the escape, his fingerprints were found on a stolen car in Ottawa. On July 20, a military information officer said that there was "no doubt" that McCauley had left the area. This claim was substantiated a month later. On August 20, a police constable in West Vancouver pulled over a vehicle while checking out a suspected car theft. After a brief struggle, the constable arrested the driver at gunpoint. A fingerprint check identified him as the elusive McCauley.

Gerald Larocque of Toronto, in Millhaven with convictions for robbery and attempted break and enter, was apprehended without incident by Montreal police in September, which left just two of the fugitives still on the run.

Charles Warren Boomer was detained by police in San Jose, California, on October 9, 1972. Boomer had been serving thirty-seven years for armed robbery and previous prison escapes. Instead of keeping a low profile after fleeing down south, he went back to his crime of choice: robbery. The OPP were quite happy to leave him in the tender care of the San Jose police. In November 1972, *The Kingston Whig-Standard* published a statement issued by spokesperson Chief Inspector A.W. Goard. "I understand that they are holding him on bail of nearly $250,000. It is better if he gets a term down there, and then we don't have to worry about him." And, best of all, "It won't cost the taxpayer in this country anything."

Boomer was either released or escaped from custody, and he went on to notoriety as a bank robber known as the Satchel Bandit, so-called because he stuffed his ill-gotten gains into a bag slung over his shoulder. He worked alone, always sporting a silver semi-automatic pistol and fleeing by car, on foot, and, on occasion, by bike. He was ultimately wanted by Canadian and U.S. authorities for a string of armed bank robberies in the late 1980s and early 1990s. Arrested in Hamilton in 1992, he pleaded guilty to twenty-two armed robberies in Canada and was sentenced to twenty-five years.

In November 1972, the last man at large, Sreto "Lucky" Dzambas, was seized by Interpol agents in Belgrade, Yugoslavia (now Serbia). He had been serving a life sentence for the crowbar murder of a Toronto restaurant worker during a bungled robbery attempt in 1970, but, as he was a Yugoslavian national, extradition seemed highly unlikely. As *The Kingston Whig-Standard* noted on November 30, however, Toronto police were hopeful that, even if he were not returned to Canada, Yugoslavian officials would deal with him and "make him serve his sentence over there. In that country life means life."

In fact, a murder conviction in Yugoslavia at the time might have terminated in something far more sinister: death by firing squad.

It did not come to that. Amid rumblings in his native country that he had not received a fair trial in Canada, Dzambas was initially sent to prison for three years, then released. In 1979, he was retried in Yugoslavia and sentenced to ten-and-a-half years for assault, even though his crimes had taken place in Canada. The saga was still ongoing in 1981. Dzambas had appealed his sentence on the grounds that he had been framed by two other defendants at his original Canadian trial.

Dzambas was the only one of the Millhaven 14 who slipped through the Canadian net. Ultimately, though, just like the others, he did not escape the clutches of the law.

A question that invariably comes up in FAQs about prisons escapes is: Where do escapees actually go? Based on data from police and media sources in the United Kingdom for the years 2015–16, a BBC investigation in 2017 found that, irrespective of the security level of the prison, the average distance travelled by fugitives before they are caught is 36 miles (57 kilometres).

This finding flies in the face of the often-expressed opinion that escapees will try to put as much distance as they possibly can between themselves and the place they have just left, and it is certainly applicable to the Millhaven 14. Nine of the fugitives were recaptured within a radius of thirty kilometres from the penitentiary.

The BBC survey also found that some offenders simply go home (which was the case with Rudolph Nuss, who was recaptured at his parents' house in Niagara-on-the-Lake), while a number of them manage to flee the country. Two of the Millhaven escapees, Boomer and Dzambas, did just that. Eventually, however, just like the rest of the escapees, both were brought to justice — Boomer in Canada and Dzambas in his native Yugoslavia.

6

A Dog's Life

Donald Kelly: From Folk Hero to *Persona Non Grata*

IN NOVEMBER 1969, TWO BODIES, BOTH WITH GUNSHOT WOUNDS TO the head, were found floating in the North River near North Bay, Ontario. After a five-and-a-half-year investigation, Donald James Kelly was arrested in Edmonton, Alberta, and returned to his hometown of North Bay. Along with two accomplices, Kelly was charged in April 1975 with the double murder of Carol Ann "Corky" MacWilliams and her brother-in-law, Jack MacWilliams.

During their preliminary hearing, the three accused — Donald Kelly, James Lavin, and Ian Rose — were locked up in the Nipissing District North Bay Jail.

Built in 1929, the North Bay Jail ushered in its first batch of inmates in November 1930. The squat, rectangular brick building with concrete trim around the front entrance contained sixty-nine cells, housing both males and females awaiting trial, sentencing, or transfer to other institutions, or serving short-term sentences of up to two years less a day.

Given that such an institution typically incarcerates the whole gamut of inmates, including serious offenders like armed robbers or murderers, the architecture of the jail proclaimed in no uncertain terms: this is a maximum-security facility. As described on the Nipissing District North Bay Jail heritage site plaque, the building had "outer walls … 26 inches thick … composed of brick, concrete and reinforced steel." Furthermore, it was touted as "fire and escape proof."

On the morning of Saturday, August 2, 1975, during a visit from his mother, Donald Kelly gave the lie to that boast.

On August 5, *The Toronto Star* shared this snippet from his bemused mom: "I was sitting in the visiting room talking to him about God and the Bible when all of a sudden he took about three jumps and away he went. I didn't know where he was going. I only know that he didn't want to be in jail."

Kelly, thirty-seven, described as five feet ten inches tall, 173 pounds in weight, and with black hair and brown eyes, had seized the moment.

He bolted across the room, punched an unarmed and unsuspecting guard, and ran out through an open door to the rear parking lot of the jail, sidestepping a grocery delivery truck as he fled. North Bay police later said that Kelly had grabbed a weapon from a truck parked outside, left there by a fellow prisoner who was serving a weekend sentence. After firing a shot to discourage the now-recovered guard and anyone else who might try to stop him, Kelly commandeered a passing car and was gone. Two days later, the abandoned car was found hidden in the bushes near North Bay Jack Garland Airport.

The public — and police — barely had time to absorb the details of his jailbreak on Saturday before learning that his initial burst of activity had been followed by a flurry of hostage taking. His first victim was a hunter from Toronto, whom he came across while walking through the woods after his stolen car broke down. On Saturday night, he seized five young people and hijacked their vehicle. By Sunday morning, Kelly's tally of hostages had risen to ten, the last four being the occupants of a cottage on Lake Talon, to the east of North Bay. After tying up his captives, Kelly reportedly drank six bottles of beer, swallowed some tranquilizers, and finally made off with some ammunition and the cottagers' car, leaving the group traumatized but unharmed.

According to the hostages, a talkative Kelly had informed them that he had a "death list" of six North Bay policemen. A police spokesman was quoted in the *Star* on August 5 as saying that he believed the threat to be "a little more sincere" than those usually aimed at police officers. "[Kelly] has said he has a score to settle with them," the official observed grimly.

Kelly also told one of the hostages that he "had nothing to lose," and that he didn't intend to go back to prison alive. "I've got the name; I might as well have the reputation," he added.

Kelly's lawyer, Richard Donnelly, was pessimistic. As recorded in *The Globe and Mail* on August 7, he said: "I doubt very much whether I'll ever see my client alive again." He feared that things were deteriorating to the point where only a miracle could prevent a deadly shootout.

By that time, Kelly was reportedly carrying an array of weapons, including three rifles — a .303 calibre, a .22 calibre equipped with a telescopic sight, and a .30-30.

North Bay police chief William Wotherspoon openly voiced his misgivings, describing Kelly in the *Star* of August 5 as "a real con artist, and … very dangerous. Right now, we don't know what to expect. He's good in the bush. He's a hunter and a fisherman and he knows how to travel in these conditions."

Underscoring police concerns were memories of an earlier manhunt in North Bay, which had spooked the community some fifty years prior. In May 1923, twenty-one-year-old Leo Rogers, a local man on parole from Kingston Penitentiary, was arrested in North Bay for illegal possession of a firearm. Somehow arming himself with a fake revolver (reportedly fashioned from an umbrella handle and a bar of soap), Rogers escaped from the local courthouse. Like Kelly, Rogers was a skilled marksman and completely at home in the bush. During a two-week reign of terror, Rogers shot and killed a plainclothes detective and an Ontario Provincial Police (OPP) officer. Police finally closed in on him on the shores of Lake Nipissing, and he was brought down in a hail of bullets. Again, like Kelly, Rogers was heavily armed: police recovered from his body a .30-30-calibre rifle, a .32-calibre revolver, and several sticks of dynamite.

In the immediate aftermath of Donald Kelly's escape, a full-scale manhunt had been launched. Armed with shotguns and semi-automatic rifles, more than 150 city and provincial police, along with tracking dogs and helicopters, took part in the search. Roadblocks were set up on all roads out of North Bay, and all traffic leaving the city was checked.

As per the August 7 *Globe* article, after more than ten sweaty hours on the job, a hot-and-bothered policeman grumbled, "He's up there laughing at us."

And, indeed, Kelly did seem to be toying with the frustrated cops. As the *Globe* put it on August 8: "Donald James Kelly has policemen following cold trails and bumping up against dead ends."

Input from the public didn't help. Reported gunshots turned out to be doors slamming, and suspects turned out to be skeet shooters, or berry pickers, or hitchhikers, or youths riding motorbikes. In one incident, fifty armed officers in bullet-proof vests stormed a house trailer about fifteen kilometres northeast of the city after receiving information that someone had been heard yelling, "What leg do you want me to shoot, the left or the right?" and "Smarten up or I'll blow your head off!" As described in the *Star* on August 7 as though it were the most natural thing in the world, the shouter turned out to be an exasperated father, disciplining his son at the end of a pointed (and possibly loaded) gun.

On August 6, a $5,000 reward was offered by the Ontario Government and the North Bay Police Commission for information leading to the fugitive's arrest. Instead of unleashing a torrent of tips, news of the reward seemed to boost the outlaw's credibility. A joke started circulating in North Bay — that come fall, hunters would be issued licences for moose, deer, bear, and Kelly. A local radio station began to play an old song called "Has Anybody Here Seen Kelly?"

Kelly was fast becoming a local folk hero.

By August 14, Kelly was up to his old tricks again: hostage taking. This time, he upped the ante, holding six adults and five children who were camping in the McConnell Lake Park area, around eighty kilometres northeast of the city.

Like a character in an American gangster movie (*Bonnie and Clyde*, perhaps?), a smiling Kelly posed for pictures holding a gun, while his hostages snapped enthusiastically away on their cameras.

After spending fifteen hours with his captives, Kelly disabled two of their vehicles and drove away in the third. The hostages claimed that Kelly had not once raised his voice. However, their captor did say that he had three sticks of dynamite in his backpack, and that, if he were cornered, he would blow himself up and take down a couple of cops with him.

As the manhunt dragged on, North Bay residents were warned to lock their doors and not admit strangers. House-to-house searches and roadblocks continued. Special protection was provided to several police officers and other members of the community who had received death threats. And Kelly was clearly thumbing his nose at the authorities: the car he stole from the campers was found abandoned near a former haunt just a few blocks from North Bay City Hall.

The police were concerned about an inflammatory "shootout mentality" that seemed to be developing in news reports about the manhunt. On August 19, the *Globe* recorded an OPP officer as stating with emphasis, "I've never been in a shooting and I don't want to be. We want him to know he can walk in and give himself up." A hopeful sign was that even though Kelly had seized hostages, he had not harmed any of them.

In the *Star* edition of August 16, Chief William Wotherspoon professed to be not too worried. "Really, North Bay has a crime rate below the national average," he said. He admitted, though, that regular police work in the city of fifty thousand was at a standstill. "Our force is devoting 100 percent of its time to the search."

On Tuesday, August 19, Kelly increased his total hostage count to twenty-three. He seized a grandfather and grandson at Crystal Falls to the west of North Bay and forced them to drive him to just outside Sudbury. The fugitive, now sporting a full black beard, was shaking badly during the drive — withdrawal symptoms, perhaps, as police believed that Kelly, a known drug user, might be very low on supplies.

After thirty days, Kelly was still on the loose, and the police were desperate for a break.

///////////////////

On August 31, railroad workers near Skead, about thirty-eight kilometres northeast of Sudbury, spotted a man with a gun walking on the Canadian National Railway tracks. The OPP dispatched a team of three from the North Bay detachment to investigate: Constable Raymond Carson and his tracker dog, Cloud II, and, riding shotgun, Constable Ted Giannini.

The two men were experienced and dependable officers, but by far the most outstanding member of the team was the one with four legs. Cloud II had a stellar resumé. The five-year-old German Shepherd had graduated with Carson from a fourteen-week training course, meeting all the requisite standards in tracking, disarming, jumping, and detecting narcotics. Over the course of his career, he and Carson had taken down 123 fugitives and located dozens of lost children and hunters.

In 1972, as you will remember, man and dog had participated in the hunt for the fourteen escapees from Millhaven Institution and, notably, had brought down Donald Oag, one of the most dangerous of the bunch. Even more memorably, Cloud dashed into an ice-fishing hut near North Bay in 1973 to confront two juvenile jailbreakers. He emerged with a loaded rifle and went back in to seize a knife. He then hunted down and disarmed a third youth. These exploits earned him an induction into the Purina Animal Hall of Fame in 1974.

Halfway through the hunt for Kelly, Carson predicted that it was just a matter of time. The police would surely get their man — alive.

So when the two men and a dog came across their quarry enjoying his lunch on the front porch of a remote hunting cabin on September 1, Carson broke into a smile.

His pleasure was short-lived. When the fugitive reached for his rifle and started to run, Carson unleashed the dog. Cloud grabbed the man's leg, and Kelly shot and killed him. Giannini responded with two shotgun blasts. Although wounded, Kelly returned his fire before disappearing into the bush.

The officers put in an urgent call for backup. Kelly, meanwhile, had circled back and taken refuge in the cabin. At around 7:00 p.m., a team of five policemen lobbed teargas canisters into the cabin and stormed in. Kelly was lying on the floor, with no weapon in sight. He offered no resistance to his arrest.

Kelly was taken to Sudbury General Hospital with three shotgun pellets in his lung and a badly broken arm. Late that night, he was reported as being in serious but not critical condition.

As revealed in the *Star* on September 2, the death of Cloud II hit Carson hard. "He was doing his work and … he's finished," he said. "He just loved police work and he was fantastic at disarming a man." But, he added, "we got him — and he's alive. I said we would."

On September 4, 1975, the headline on page 1 of the *Star* read, "Dog gets hero's burial as mourning police form guard of honor [sic]." People came from as far afield as Toronto, Timmins, and Wawa to join the crowd of 350 paying their respects to the canine hero. They stood in silence as the flag-draped box was carried to the grave, positioned between the flagpoles at the OPP headquarters in North Bay. Present were a Burks Falls mother and her two-year-old daughter. Some months previously, the toddler had been rescued by Carson and Cloud after wandering off into thick bush.

Media reports of Cloud's death and burial ignited a firestorm of letters to the editor. Between September 12 and September 26, many of them landed in *The Toronto Star*'s mailroom.

By far the largest number of letters were in praise of the dog. Typical was this extract: "The main reason the funeral of Cloud II received such publicity is that a creature of a supposedly lower order than man proved itself noble, giving up its life in the process. Families and friends of our brave protectors owe a debt of deep gratitude to this animal, and there is nothing wrong with their expressing it publicly."

And regarding criticism of the cost of Cloud's funeral, one person wrote: "Kelly's bid for freedom cost upwards of $80,000, not to mention what was lost by the business community in the North due to an absence of tourists because he was at large. What is the cost of Cloud II's funeral compared to that?" (In fact, the manhunt cost a whopping $98,287.84, of which $92,955 was paid by the province in March 1976.)

One correspondent, referring to herself as a one-time owner and trainer of German Shepherd guard dogs, challenged claims that such animals are intrinsically vicious: "An animal who can be trusted to locate a frightened and possibly hysterical child is unlikely to attack without cause or prior warning. In fact all these dogs are trained to a system of warning visibly first (growling, showing of teeth), then immobilizing (by cornering or knocking down and watching the suspect), and finally, as a last resort, by actually biting."

A scattering of letters described the gratitude lavished upon the dog as inappropriate: One writer was "dismayed" by coverage of the funeral; another, a seventeen-year-old youth, was "disgusted with the amount of press and hero worship.... This was a dog trained to be vicious in certain situations. Is that heroic? I think not."

German Shepherd Cloud II and his trainer and handler, Constable (later Staff Sergeant) Ray Carson, both of the Ontario Provincial Police's canine unit. Cloud was shot and killed by North Bay escapee Donald Kelly.

Something glossed over in all those impassioned letters was dryly noted by former North Bay police chief George Berrigan in *Police Stories: Tales from a Small-Town Cop*: "It seemed to some that the public outrage over the killing of the police tracking dog was greater than that for the murders of Jack and Corky MacWilliams."

///////////////////

On January 28, 1976, Donald Kelly, dressed in a neat grey suit and with his arm still in a sling, was arraigned in provincial court on twenty-eight new charges to add to the two for murder he had already racked up: fifteen for forcible confinement, eight for kidnapping, three for armed robbery, one for escaping from prison, and one for possessing a weapon dangerous to the public peace.

Kelly was not charged for killing Cloud. Interestingly, the *Canadian Justice for Animals in Service Act*, also called Quanto's Law after an Edmonton police dog stabbed to death while pursuing a suspect, was enacted in 2015. This amendment to the Criminal Code ensures that offenders who harm law-enforcement, military, and service animals are held fully accountable. Today, Kelly could have faced up to five years in jail for shooting Cloud.

The Ontario Supreme Court ordered that the trial of Kelly and his co-accused in the 1969 murders of Carol Ann "Corky" MacWilliams, aged twenty, and her twenty-seven-year-old brother-in-law, John MacWilliams, be moved to Toronto. The court also ordered that Ian Rose and James Lavin be tried separately from Kelly.

In his opening address at Kelly's murder trial in April 1976, the Crown attorney told the court that the MacWilliamses had both been executed "in typical gangland fashion" before their bodies were dumped in the North River in November 1969.

The slayings had reportedly been preceded by "a happy party," attended by Corky MacWilliams, who chatted cordially with her alleged murderers. Large quantities of drugs and booze were consumed, and Kelly and Lavin entertained the crowd by whipping out two revolvers and taking pot-shots at a ceramic ornament. After MacWilliams left the party, Kelly, Lavin, and

Rose headed out, ostensibly to get more beer. They returned sometime later without the beer. It was alleged that they had, instead, lured the two victims to their deaths. At least one slug retrieved in the house had been fired from the same gun as that used in the slayings.

Kelly's case was not helped by the testimony of two former girlfriends. According to the *Globe* on April 16, Patricia Fragomeni, who described herself as a reformed prostitute and heroin addict, told the court that she'd seen Kelly on his return to the party on November 16, 1969. He had blood stains on his shirt and admitted that he had taken part in the murders. Nicole Gladu, who had lived with Kelly in Edmonton in 1974, testified that he'd confessed to shooting Corky MacWilliams after James Lavin had killed Jack. Gladu's testimony hinted at a possible motive for the crimes: "He said Mrs. MacWilliams had threatened to tell the police about something he had done."

It took the jury twenty-two hours to come to a verdict: Guilty.

On April 23, Kelly was sentenced to life imprisonment. The following day, the *Globe* recorded his furious reaction to both the verdict and his sentence. He insisted that he had been framed and accused his erstwhile girlfriends of having accepted bribes of $5,000 to lie about him. "I just hope they choke on it," he said.

Despite speculation that charges for his jailbreak and subsequent hostage-taking spree might be dropped, Kelly was sentenced in October 1976 to eight years, after pleading guilty to seven charges relating to his escape.

Lavin, thirty-seven, and twenty-six-year-old Rose got off much more lightly. Or, as some suggest, it might be more accurate to say that they got away with it completely: In December 1976, they were both found not guilty of the gangland-style killings. Perhaps their acquittal had something to do with the fact that, unlike the chatty Kelly, they had managed to avoid sharing the gory details of their criminous activities with any of their friends.

Cloud II, still esteemed in police circles as the only OPP dog ever killed in the line of duty, had originally been buried on the grounds of the OPP District Headquarters in North Bay. But when the headquarters moved to a new site in 2011, his remains were relocated to the OPP Museum in Orillia — local officers did not want to "leave him behind" — with a touching ceremony to mark the occasion.

In 2014, seventy-eight-year-old former staff sergeant Ray Carson passed away in North Bay. During his thirty-two years with the OPP, he was the handler of three successive Clouds — I, II, and III — and for many years he coordinated the OPP K9 unit.

Kelly's end predated that of his human adversary. In 2009, at the age of seventy-one, he died of natural causes in British Columbia — unsurprisingly, still behind bars.

7

"Le Grand Gangster"

Leaving a Trail of Murder and Mayhem on Both Sides of the Atlantic

JACQUES RENÉ MESRINE, KNOWN TO HIS ADMIRERS AS "LE GRAND Jacques" and to his detractors as "Le grand gangster," was born in December 1936 into a solid middle-class family in Clichy, a suburb in northwestern Paris. Although Mesrine's father claimed that his boy had strayed from the straight and narrow after serving in the 1950s with French troops in the brutal Algerian War (for which Mesrine was awarded several medals for bravery), there were strong signals in his youth that he was not destined to become an upstanding French citizen. To illustrate: he was expelled from a prestigious private Catholic school for beating up the principal.

The skills he acquired in the army were further honed by his involvement in l'Organisation de l'armée secrète or OAS, a French terrorist group dedicated to maintaining France's colonial hold over Algeria. Mesrine became a firearms expert and probably a weapons smuggler and extortionist. He cultivated useful connections with criminal networks that could supply false or stolen documents on demand. He also developed a supreme disregard for human life. In fact, he would later claim in his memoir, *L'instinct de mort*, to have murdered thirty-nine people, although he may well have inflated the number.

After leaving the army, Mesrine worked briefly as a salesman, a job he found crushingly boring. Becoming a burglar was just a soupçon more exciting but far more lucrative. In 1965, however, an incursion into the home of the governor of Palma, Mallorca, led to a conviction and jail sentence. Mesrine had a wife and three kids at the time; his jail term would spell the end of the marriage.

By 1968, things had become exceptionally hot for Mesrine in his native country, and he prudently decided to seek out quieter pastures. What better place to relocate to than the Canadian province of Quebec, where there would be no language difficulties, and where there existed a flourishing criminal community for him to tap into?

By the time Mesrine landed in Montreal with his latest paramour, Jeanne Schneider (nicknamed Janou), in tow, he had stacked up quite an impressive portfolio of crimes — extortion, burglaries, armed robberies — although it would take another decade or so for him to reach his full potential.

In addition to his more nefarious qualifications, Mesrine had quite a flair in the kitchen. In March 1969, he found gainful employment as the chauffeur and chef of fifty-eight-year-old Georges Deslauriers, described on July 17 in *The Toronto Daily Star* as "a crippled millionaire wholesale vegetable dealer," at his Mont-Saint-Hilaire estate just outside Montreal. However, a vicious altercation between Schneider, who was employed as housemaid, and Deslauriers's long-serving gardener put an end to this legitimate and extremely cushy job. Mesrine and Schneider were both sacked.

Stung by their dismissal, Mesrine decided that if he couldn't extract money from his former employer by fair means, he would use foul: kidnapping plus a ransom demand. After all, with his disability, Deslauriers seemed such an easy mark.

"LE GRAND GANGSTER"

The caper was a total bust.

According to Michel Laentz in his "true history" of Mesrine, the timid and inexperienced young hoodlum that Mesrine and Schneider enlisted to watch over Deslauriers in their rented Montreal apartment became alarmed when the latter seemed to be gasping for breath, and he bolted. When Mesrine and Schneider returned to the apartment after mailing off a ransom demand of $200,000 to Deslauriers's brother, the street was teeming with police and there was an ambulance parked in front of the building. Deslauriers had struggled free of his bonds and called through the window for help.

Not Le grand Jacques's finest hour.

He and Schneider fled to the small tourist centre of Percé in the Gaspé region of Quebec, where they took refuge in a modest motel. Toward the end of June 1969, the couple left the region and slipped across the United States border. They were arrested two weeks later near Texarkana, Texas, and extradited.

Back in Canada, Mesrine and Schneider learned that they were facing murder as well as kidnapping charges — the body of the motel's proprietor, Évelyne Lebouthillier, had been discovered after their departure. She had been strangled. The pair had been identified by witnesses, and their fingerprints were found at the motel.

In spite of Mesrine's vehement denials that he had anything to do with this particular killing, September 1969 found him and Schneider awaiting a preliminary hearing in the Percé jail. In *L'instinct de mort*, Mesrine describes how he threatened the night guard with a homemade knife before relieving him of his keys. Ever dutiful, he then freed Schneider, and they ran off, leaving both the guard and the matron of the jail locked up in separate cells. The twosome was not at large for long. The following morning, police found them, shivering and hopelessly lost, lying side by side in the woods near Percé.

At Mesrine and Schneider's murder trial in early 1971, claims by members of the murdered woman's family that jewellery found in the couple's possession belonged to the victim were convincingly refuted. To the indignation of the judge, whom Mesrine described as "odious," the jury found both of them not guilty. Mesrine, however, had earlier been sentenced to eleven years for kidnapping, armed robbery, and escaping custody, and Schneider, found guilty of the same offences, received a sentence of five-and-a-half years. Schneider was later extradited to France, and the couple would never meet again.

Mesrine served little more than a year in a Canadian prison before making a move.

On August 21, 1972, he was one of six prisoners who breezed out of the special correction unit of the forbidding stone Saint-Vincent-de-Paul Penitentiary in Laval, Quebec. Also known as the "old Pen," it dated back to 1873 — the sole francophone correctional institution in Canada until it stopped operating as a prison in the 1980s, and, after Kingston Pen, the oldest.

The day after the breakout, readers of *The Globe and Mail* were given the lowdown. The paper quoted the warden of the penitentiary as describing the special correction unit as "maximum security detention quarters for extremely dangerous men. All have either been involved in other jail breaks or have been in fights with other prisoners and guards." All were serving sentences of between ten and twenty-five years.

During a recreational period, the sextet (two of them bare chested) simply used a pair of pliers to snip their way through the perimeter fences made of double wire mesh and topped with barbed wire.

Mesrine's sidekick was Quebecker Jean-Paul Mercier, aged twenty-eight, who had been serving a twenty-four-year sentence for a hodgepodge of crimes ranging from armed robbery to attempted murder. Mercier had previously broken free in 1971 from the Archambault Institution in Sainte-Anne-des-Plaines, Quebec, by hacking through cement blocks in his cell. On that occasion, he was at large for just one day.

Despite an extensive manhunt by prison guards and the Sûreté du Québec (SQ) or Quebec provincial police, armed with shotguns and rifles and assisted by an SQ helicopter, no trace of the six escapees was found in the area around Saint-Vincent-de-Paul. It was later reported that the group had fled in "two late-model cars."

When questioned, penitentiary guards were at a complete loss. No one had witnessed the breakout, not even the men posted in two lookout towers.

According to the lengthy *Globe* report of August 22, one guard had reported seeing several individuals outside the prison wall but was not sure whether or not they were inmates. "It was only [when a head count was taken] we were sure the six had escaped," said the warden.

Solicitor General Jean-Pierre Goyer wasn't buying it. How could six men escape with such insouciance from a special unit that had been specifically designed to house hardened criminals and known escape artists? "I'm sick and tired of hearing authorities say it's because [guards] haven't got enough security gadgets," he fumed. "The guards should have fired several warning shots when they spotted the movements in the bush and fired at the escapees if they failed to stop."

A sculpture outside Saint-Vincent-de-Paul Penitentiary in Laval, Quebec, established in 1873, which served for more than a hundred years as the only francophone correctional institution in Canada. French gangster Jacques Mesrine, who escaped from this facility in 1972, referred to it as a place of hatred and suffering.

To celebrate their freedom, Team Mesrine-Mercier hit two Quebec City credit unions in quick succession, which netted them the tidy sum of $13,300.

Then came the events of September 3, 1972.

Instead of being sent to cover their usual beat at Viau in eastern Laval, two local police officers were dispatched to patrol the environs of Saint-Vincent-de-Paul, where prisoners were enjoying a family day. At around 1:30 p.m., the officers were alerted by penitentiary guards to what was later described as a "voiture louche" about 150 metres from their patrol car. As they approached the "dodgy car," they found it to be a rather ordinary brown Dodge. But, as one of the officers explained to *Le Journal de Montreal* in 2019, "It had a scarf hanging from its antenna. I told myself that this was not normal and that it was perhaps a signal to the inmates."

How right he was.

The Dodge sped away, with the officers in hot pursuit. After a brief chase, the vehicle screeched to a halt. Within moments the two occupants coolly stepped out, pulled out semi-automatic weapons, and sprayed the police car with bullets. The cruiser crashed into a ditch, and, with bullets whizzing around them, the policemen dived for cover. They were saved from certain death when penitentiary guards in a separate car opened fire on the assailants, who then fled.

After the incident, the officers learned that rumours had been swirling about of an imminent jailbreak. Furthermore, the abortive escape had been orchestrated from the outside by those two machine-gun-wielding bandits in the Dodge — who turned out to be none other than Jacques Mesrine and his devoted acolyte, Jean-Paul Mercier.

According to Edward Butts in his book *Line of Fire*, Mesrine and Mercier had rented several apartments in Montreal to use as hideouts and had stocked them with food. And, in addition to their own firepower, they had brought along extra pistols to lob over the exercise yard fence. Their aim? To liberate jailbirds from the hated maximum-security wing.

Although the attempt was foiled, "conspiring in the escape of other prisoners" was added to the litany of charges (kidnapping, robbery, attempted murder, murder, escaping legal custody) already littering Mesrine's rap sheet in Quebec.

Just how lucky the woefully uninformed and under-armed policemen had been to survive the attack emerged a few days later.

When forest rangers Médéric Côté of Plessisville and Ernest Saint-Pierre of Daveluyville failed to return from their day shift on September 10, their families were not, initially, overly concerned. It was not unusual for rangers to work overtime if circumstances required it. When they were still missing at five o'clock the following morning, however, their superior officer raised the alarm with the SQ.

The men had reportedly been investigating gunfire — poachers, perhaps? — in the vicinity of Saint-Louis-de-Blandford, some one hundred kilometres to the southwest of Quebec City. The search began there. By 9:00 a.m., the rangers' truck was located. The bodies of the two men were found in the bushes nearby. They had both been shot six times.

Analysis of bullets and bullet casings found in a nearby clearing provided homicide detectives with a direct link to Mesrine and Mercier, who, it later emerged, had come to the forest with Mercier's girlfriend for a picnic and some target practice. They had encountered the rangers on their way out of the area, with tragic consequences for the two innocent men.

After spending a few weeks in Montreal, Mesrine and Mercier conceded that it was perhaps time to move on. The two men made their way to Venezuela. But Interpol was on their trail. They decided to part ways, and Mercier returned to Quebec.

Mesrine made his way back to la belle France in early 1973, where, to his great satisfaction, he was soon crowned both Public Enemy Number One and the Man of a Thousand Faces, the latter title reflecting his supreme mastery of the art of disguise. He was also celebrated by the populace as a kind of folk hero. He cultivated this image, as noted in a *Montreal Gazette* story in November 1979, writing: "I am the enemy only of banks ... I never attack Grandma or Little Red Riding Hood."

"Judge used as shield by escaper," marvelled *The Globe and Mail* on June 7, 1973. In court in Compiègne, France, for a cheque-fraud case, Mesrine collected a gun that accomplices had secreted in a men's washroom, and, after threatening to kill the judge, calmly walked out of the courtroom, using the judge as a buffer. A getaway car was waiting for him outside.

By September 1973, he had been recaptured. He was sent to La Santé Prison in Paris to serve out a twenty-year sentence for armed robbery.

///////////////

Although the words "LIBERTÉ ÉGALITÉ FRATERNITÉ" are emblazoned in bold upper-case letters above one of the entrances to La Santé Prison, liberty is not a word usually associated with this bleak establishment. Located right in the heart of the French capital, La Santé is regarded as one of the world's most secure prisons. It generally figures just after Colorado's dreaded "Alcatraz of the Rockies," ADX Florence, on any list of institutions that are well-nigh impossible to escape from. Once you're in, you're in. Period.

La Santé, built between 1861 and 1867, with its hub-and-spoke architecture reflecting the penological philosophy of the Eastern State or Pennsylvania model developed in the United States in the early 1800s — individual cells with strict oversight and severely limited interaction between prisoners — initially contained five hundred cells. Over time, this number more than doubled, and, until a massive refit was undertaken between 2014 and 2019, the population in this notoriously overcrowded establishment hovered above the two-thousand mark.

In 1970, a "quartier de haute sécurité" (QHS) was opened. This was a super-maximum-security unit within the prison reserved for inmates who were either presumed or recognized as dangerous and considered a flight risk.

It was common knowledge in 1978 that Jacques Mesrine, cloistered in that super-repressive wing, was planning to break out.

The odds were against him — in the 101 years since the fortress prison was inaugurated, only one prisoner had ever escaped. That was back in 1927, when, thirteen days after Royalist leader and newspaper editor Léon Daudet was imprisoned, one of his jokester colleagues at his paper took to the telephone to mimic the voice of a senior government official and order Daudet's release.

But Mesrine plainly thumbed his nose at the odds.

It played out like a scene from a gritty French thriller. On May 8, 1978, Mesrine met with one of his lawyers in a windowless antechamber, supervised by a prison guard keeping close watch through a soundproof glass door. When the guard inexplicably complied with Mesrine's request to fetch a legal file from his cell, Mesrine leaped onto a table, tore off the cover of a ventilator duct, and grabbed two weapons and a teargas grenade that had been secreted there.

Mesrine's partner in crime this time was fellow inmate François Besse — like him, an accomplished escape artist. Together, they had planned the break to the last meticulous detail and had invited a third bandit, lifer Carman Rives, along for the ride.

A generous squirt of teargas disabled a guard outside Besse's cell, and within minutes both Besse and Rives were free. The trio overpowered several guards, donned their uniforms, and, with the aid of a strategically placed ladder and a grappling iron, they scaled an outer wall and swung down a rope on the other side. Before he reached the ground, however, the luckless Rives was shot dead by a guard; Mesrine and Besse drove off in a car they commandeered at gunpoint.

Following this mind-boggling breakout, Le grand gangster spent the next eighteen months leading the increasingly frustrated police in a disturbing dance. Becoming more and more daring, he carried out raids on a casino in Deauville and a bank in Paris, in each case revealing his identity to the shocked cashiers. In July 1979, he collected a cool $1.4 million ransom for the release of a kidnapped real estate magnate. Invalidating his claim of being a modern-day Robin Hood who only targeted banks, in September of that year he abducted and tortured a journalist who had had the audacity to accuse him of cheating on his friends.

But, at last, grimly determined law-enforcement agents were on his tail, managing to trace his whereabouts through close surveillance of a former cellmate.

When Jacques Mesrine, accompanied by his latest paramour Sylvie Jeanjacquot and her poodle, climbed into his BMW on November 2, 1979, and set off from his apartment in Paris for a weekend in the country, he had reached the pinnacle of his reprehensible career. On his resumé were multiple bank robberies, kidnappings, murders, escapes from custody, clashes on both sides of the Atlantic with law enforcement officers (often excruciatingly humiliating for the latter), as well as a couple of well-received books and many self-aggrandizing interviews. The master of disguise was sporting a false beard and a curly haired wig at the time.

As they approached the Porte de Clignancourt on the northern fringes of the capital, their car was cut off by several vehicles, including a canvas-covered truck carrying a clutch of police sharpshooters. The shooters let fly.

Mesrine, often called "the French Dillinger," would die like Dillinger, the notorious Depression-era American gangster.

He was riddled with eighteen bullets, the fusillade bringing to an end two bloody decades of murder and mayhem. Jeanjacquot was seriously injured, after taking a bullet to the head. According to police, she owed her life to her poodle, who was killed by a bullet that would otherwise have torn through her stomach.

In an article on November 5, 1979, *The Montreal Gazette* provided its readers with a full description of the takedown, noting that after the event, the French prime minister had sent his "very hearty congratulations" to the police. The media had echoed this point of view — with the sole exception of one "leftist daily" newspaper. Commenting on television footage showing grinning police officers standing beside Mesrine's crumpled body, *Liberation* opined that the ambush was "aimed purely and simply at wiping him out. Naturally no official voice was raised in protest."

The police were defiant. "We knew he had grenades in his car," said the commissioner. "We could not allow him to use them against our men. We had to fire first."

Police who swarmed into Mesrine's Paris apartment found handguns, a submachine gun, two shotguns, smoke grenades, a gas mask, and some of the million-plus ransom dollars he had scored for the kidnapping in July.

They also found an audiotape containing a message for his girlfriend.

With his signature bravado, as revealed in *The Globe and Mail* on November 5, Mesrine signed off, saying: "My dear Sylvie, when you hear this recording, I will be dead, gunned down by the police. But I regret nothing. I lived the life I wanted, a full life ... one day perhaps we'll meet again, certainly not in paradise but maybe in hell."

8

Marking Time

The Life and Times of the Legendary Stopwatch Gang

WHEN THE AUTHORS OF THE CANADIAN EDITION OF QUIRKY *The Book of Lists* were looking for an expert to rattle off the ten toughest prisons in North America, they could hardly have made a better choice than Stephen Reid. After all, they noted, by the time their book was published in 2005, Reid had spent close to twenty years in more than twenty prisons in the United States and Canada and had escaped from several. He was also a member of the storied Stopwatch Gang, who, in the 1970s and '80s, kept bamboozled law enforcement officers on both sides of the forty-ninth parallel on the hop and the public glued to their newspapers, radios, and TV screens.

In December 2005, *Maclean's* published an excerpt from the book in an article titled "Stephen Reid's 10 toughest prisons in North America."

Reid's top three: the now-shuttered United States Penitentiary, Alcatraz Island in Northern California ("Any list of tough prisons has to begin with the Granddaddy of them all — The Rock."); United States Penitentiary, Marion in Illinois ("I spent four years there in the early '80s after it became a lockdown joint, a place where we went to the showers wearing handcuffs."); and Ontario's own Kingston Penitentiary ("I once got talking with an old swamp convict in Pensecola [sic], Florida, and he went all wide-eyed at the mention of Kingston Penitentiary, saying to me, 'You did time in that place?'").

Reid had spent nine years in Millhaven (number four on his list), where an Indigenous fellow con told him that "the prison was built on an Indian burial ground and was therefore cursed to forever remain a place of deep and abiding human misery"; eleven days in Arizona's Maricopa County Jail, where he slept in "a bullpen with one open toilet for sixty people"; a "record-hot summer" in Terre Haute, Indiana; and a chunk of time in number eight on his list, Oklahoma State Penitentiary in McAlester ("Oklahoma farm boys moonlighting as prison guards made it abundantly clear they didn't like us come-from-away city types.").

Stephen Douglas Reid was of Irish and Ojibwa stock, born on March 13, 1950, in the small mining town of Massey, Ontario. His father was an accountant and his mother a teacher's aide, and they provided Reid and his eight siblings with a decent upbringing. Reid was a bright and talented youth, until he discovered drugs and his life took a grim turn. By his late teens he had become a school dropout, a stoner, and a gun-toting thief.

At the age of twenty-two, Reid netted himself ten years for armed bank robbery in the medium-security Warkworth Institution, located in the municipality of Trent Hills, Ontario. Once free of drugs and guns, Reid excelled, and he was soon chosen to be the prison's sports director.

In October 1973, eighteen months after landing in Warkworth, Reid was given a day pass to attend a crash course on fitness programming for inmates.

He was not, however, destined to launch a new career as a health instructor.

On the way back to prison that evening, he persuaded his two escorts, totally against the rules, to stop off at a Chinese restaurant. Excusing himself partway through the meal, ostensibly for a bathroom break, he clambered out of a window and into a getaway car idling on the roadway. As noted by Greg Weston in his rollicking book *The Stopwatch Gang*, this prompted Reid's prison social worker to add a footnote to Reid's (up till then glowing) inmate assessment report: "Trustworthiness: okay until he escaped."

It was while hiding out in Ottawa after his escape that Reid met up with two local lawbreakers.

The first of these was charming, articulate, impeccably dressed Patrick Michael Mitchell, widely regarded as a natural leader. Mitchell was born in Ottawa in June 1942, the youngest of seven children. In his memoir, *This Bank Robber's Life: The Life and Fast Times of Patrick "Paddy" Mitchell*, he describes his parents as having been "hardworking, relatively honest, and mostly loving." Although he doesn't directly accuse them of prepping him for a life of crime, he does suggest that they were morally slippery. For example, his father would come home from work every day with his lunch pail stuffed with objects pilfered from his employer, to which his mother made no protest. Nor was his father averse to picking up items at suspiciously reduced prices, with the stock comment: "The guy told me that they fell off a truck."

As a youth, Paddy Mitchell was in constant trouble with the law for relatively minor offences such as fighting or stealing or loitering, and from the age of fourteen he was in and out of a juvenile training school in Guelph. Unrepentant on his release at age eighteen, he "chose to be a crook," and, with a band of like-minded youths, "stole anything that hadn't been nailed down."

Things seemed to turn around for Mitchell when, at nineteen, he fell in love and got married. The couple had a son, and, for the next ten years, Mitchell claimed to have led an exemplary life.

Then, "things just seemed to go awry."

Mitchell lost his job after a bitter strike at his workplace, and, with Christmas around the corner, he was unexpectedly cash-strapped. At that low point, he received a surprise telephone call from a casual acquaintance, Lionel James Wright. As described by Mitchell, Wright, living with his mother at the time, was an "unattractive" introvert who generally shunned human contact. Wright proved to be exceptionally fond of Mitchell, though, and he was blessed with an amazing gift of attention to detail. He was working as the night clerk for a large trucking company, and he had spotted a couple of surplus cases of Mitchell's favourite whisky in a consignment. He offered to steal them to cheer his buddy up.

This was the thin edge of the wedge. For the next couple of years, Wright plundered whatever he could from his company, with Mitchell happily fencing the stolen goods. It was too good to last — Wright was eventually fired, although, despite truckloads of circumstantial evidence, his employers couldn't actually pin anything on him.

With that trusty cash cow milked to death and the spoils squandered, Mitchell, ever the entrepreneur, cast around for other opportunities.

This is where Stephen Reid stepped in. Granted, his drug habit would make him a somewhat unreliable associate, but he did have other useful attributes: to wit, nerves of steel and extensive experience as an armed robber. And so, a partnership was born.

After about a year of moderately successful thievery in the Ottawa area, Mitchell was hungry for "the one, BIG score."

He was greatly interested to learn that shipments of gold were regularly brought into the Ottawa airport on Air Canada flights. And what a stroke of luck! Drinking pal and petty thief Gary Coutanche just happened to be a baggage handler at the airport. Coutanche jumped at the prospect of the sizable $100,000 windfall promised by Mitchell.

The outcome of this joint venture was trumpeted in headlines in *The Ottawa Citizen* of April 18, 1974 — "Airport bandits escape with $165,000 in gold." The *Citizen* had its numbers wrong; the amount quoted was the insured value. The actual value of the six gold bars carted off by the robbers was around $750,000, with a value of well over $4 million today, making it the biggest gold heist in Canadian history up till then.

This far surpassed the existing record held by Ken Leishman, set in Winnipeg in 1966. Leishman's crew had scored just $385,000-worth of gold bars, which would have a current value of around $3.5 million. Did Leishman, who would have been in prison at the time, get to know about the Ottawa job? Did he resent being upstaged? One can only speculate.

It is worthwhile noting, though, that the gold bar was raised to new and dizzying heights in April 2023, when thieves coolly drove away from Toronto's Pearson International Airport with over $20 million in gold bullion and nearly $2 million in U.S. bank notes. A year later, most of the perpetrators were apprehended, but the bulk of the ill-gotten spoils has not been — and probably never will be — recovered.

The details of the audacious 1974 Ottawa airport heist soon flashed around the world. Just before midnight on April 17, the lone security guard in charge of the gold shipment at the cargo terminal received a (bogus) phone call instructing him to allow an Air Canada worker to collect some vitally needed supplies. Cue Stephen Reid. Dressed in an Air Canada uniform, he entered, held up the guard at gunpoint, disarmed him, handcuffed him to a pipe, and covered his head with a canvas bag. Then he sawed off the padlock securing the door of the wire cage where the cargo was stored and wheeled the bullion out on a cart. Wright was waiting in a stolen green station wagon. Police set up roadblocks after the hysterical guard was discovered by cleaners at around 12:15 a.m., but the robbers were long gone.

Reid decamped to the States. After running out of money, he somewhat foolishly returned to Kingston, where he freely shared stories about his life as an armed robber. By December 1974, he was back under lock and key.

Honour among thieves may have been the watchword of the Stopwatch Gang, but the principle did not extend to Gary Coutanche. Despite Mitchell's warnings, Coutanche started spending lavishly after the heist. The police suspected that this was an inside job, and it wasn't hard to follow the dots. Ensnared by the cops and infuriated at receiving only $10,000 of the generous payoff he had been promised, Coutanche ratted on his erstwhile associates.

With insufficient evidence linking the gang to the bullion theft, the authorities bided their time. In February 1975, their patience paid off. Coutanche told police that Mitchell had asked him to slip a suitcase through customs. The bag was found to be stuffed with cocaine.

Reid was already in jail; now Mitchell and Wright were on the hot seat. They were both arrested and sentenced to seventeen years for drug trafficking.

In the summer of 1976, Mitchell and Reid were shipped off to Millhaven, while Wright was housed in the Ottawa-Carleton Detention Centre. As it happened, Wright was in the recreation yard when, with help from outside, six armed and dangerous inmates escaped by cutting through the two chain-link fences. When the criminals piled into a getaway car, Wright quietly and opportunistically joined them. It didn't take long for them to spot the stranger in their midst, and they threw him out.

The perpetrators of this unkind act soon got their comeuppance: by the following day, the sextet was back in the slammer. Wright, however, was not. The media admiringly dubbed him "The Ghost" because of his talent to simply vanish. Reid was quoted in *The Atavist Magazine* in 2015 as saying that "Lionel could be somewhere all night and people wouldn't notice. He was always part of the wallpaper." This time, he slipped away to Florida.

In 1977, Mitchell was sentenced to three more years for possession of the stolen gold — prior to his arrest, police had wiretapped his phone, and he had been overheard talking about the sale of gold bricks. Only two of those bricks, incidentally, were ever recovered.

On trial later that year, Reid, who had been IDed by the Ottawa airport security guard, was convicted of armed robbery for the gold heist. A sentence of ten years was added to the time he was currently serving for his prior armed robbery conviction.

Reid and Mitchell remained mired in that cesspit of abuse, aggression, and violent unrest — Millhaven. Desperate to escape, they signed on for several abortive schemes. One of these saw an escapee shot to death when attempting to climb over a fence. A far more ambitious effort, which consisted of laboriously hand-digging a tunnel under the tennis court, failed when the blacktop sagged during a heatwave, exposing the full course of the tunnel that had taken months to dig.

The only way out, the pals concluded, was to be transferred to a more forgiving environment. To that end, Mitchell became a model inmate and fitness freak. For his part, Reid enrolled in a hairdressing program, which, as he discovered to his great delight, could only be completed at Joyceville Institution.

Joyceville, a federal correctional facility located in rural Ontario to the northeast of Kingston, was definitely *not* on the list of North America's toughest.

When what was referred to as Canada's first "medium-minimum" penitentiary opened in 1959, *The Globe and Mail* was wildly enthusiastic. With fresh food, recreational facilities galore, television in the common rooms at night — and *The Globe and Mail* delivered daily! — it was, in short, "just about the ultimate in gracious prison living."

It was Canada's very first penitentiary with no boundary walls.

As the paper reported, the warden told a bunch of hugely impressed reporters at a slap-up lunch in December of that year, "We hope it works."

It did not.

By August 1961, in light of the increasing number of escapes from Kingston-area prisons such as Joyceville, Collins Bay, and the Kingston Prison for Women (twenty-five breakouts year to date as opposed to twelve in all of 1960), plans were afoot to build a perimeter fence around Joyceville, and by November of that year, Joyceville, smarting from twelve additional escapes, had morphed into a medium-security prison.

Flash forward to Millhaven in fall 1978, when Reid's fervent wish to get the hell out of the hellhole was finally granted. He received a transfer to Joyceville to complete his hairstyling course. Mitchell, due to his "exemplary behaviour and participation in social programs," was soon permitted to follow.

On August 15, 1979, the warden allowed Reid, accompanied by a guard, to visit a hairdressing salon in Kingston. On the way back, Reid persuaded the guard to stop for lunch.

Michael Leonard, who joined the Toronto (Don) Jail as a rookie in 1991 and ended up as the last security manager before the jail was decommissioned in 2013, describes the interaction between correctional officers and inmates as a "game of cat and mouse." Inmates are focused on beating the system. If an opportunity comes up, they will take it. Guards have to think like them to beat them at the game.

Clearly, Reid's escort did not keep this guiding principle in mind, nor did he know, or recall, what had happened back in 1973 when Reid was allowed out of Warkworth to attend a fitness program.

"One that got away." On an outing from Joyceville Institution in August 1979, Stephen Reid walked away from a guard during a lunch stop at a Kingston seafood restaurant.

The menu was different (Chinese food last time; fish and chips this time), but the modus operandi was similar: excusing himself from the table for a bathroom break, Reid simply walked out the door of the restaurant, leaving his escort no doubt cursing himself for his own gullibility.

When it came to springing Mitchell, the ploy that had worked so brilliantly for Reid was definitely not on the table. The two pals had come up with a much more spectacular, and exceptionally dangerous, plan, which came together three months after Reid's escape.

On November 15, Mitchell went for a long run, then drank a bottle of water in which he had previously soaked a whole pack of tobacco. "Unbeknownst to me," Mitchell wrote in his memoir, "it was enough nicotine to kill an elephant!"

With all the symptoms of cardiac arrest — he recalls "flopping around … like a fish out of water" — Mitchell was rushed to the Hotel Dieu Hospital in Kingston. He never got there: just outside the hospital, the ambulance crew was accosted by two bogus paramedics (Reid and Wright), who spirited away the seemingly moribund patient. For two days, Mitchell seesawed between unconsciousness and violent spasms of vomiting. Reid began to wonder nervously if he would soon have a dead body to dispose of.

But Mitchell was made of sterner stuff. It took him a week to recover; the day after that, they were all safely in the United States.

Americans, familiar with homegrown bandits like Butch Cassidy and the Sundance Kid, would now suffer a foreign invasion of epic proportions. Starting in Florida then moving on to California, the three Canadians soon hit their stride. To the fury of state and local police, as well as the Federal Bureau of Investigation (FBI), they engaged in a series of meticulously planned and swiftly executed armed bank robberies. One member of the gang (some reports credit Reid, others Mitchell) was sometimes observed wearing a stopwatch round his neck to ensure that each caper took no longer than two minutes flat, earning them the moniker "the Stopwatch Gang." They were described as unfailingly polite, and, to their credit, although they always brandished weapons (even Uzis on occasion), they never used them.

In the witty words of Greg Weston: "As the loot rolled in, the champagne got colder, the Scotch got older, the cigars got longer, the drugs got purer, the dinner tabs got more outrageous, and their tips got them celebrity status wherever they went."

By some estimates, they stole as much as $15 million Canadian (roughly equivalent to $57 million today) from as many as a hundred banks during the course of their nefarious career. San Diego was a particularly rewarding spot. After several smaller hits there, they lifted a remarkable $283,000 in cash from a Bank of America branch in September 1980.

This was to be their undoing. A rare slip-up by Wright led to the discovery of the gang's discarded paraphernalia (wigs, false beards, money wrappers, and the like) in a dumpster, and help from an obliging snitch led the FBI to their hideout in Sedona, Arizona. There, the operatives triumphantly managed to locate and arrest two-thirds of the gang. Mitchell was nowhere to be found.

Wright and Reid ended up with sentences of ten years apiece. Wright was initially sent to a maximum-security federal prison in Kansas. He received a transfer to Millhaven in 1984 but was eventually moved to medium-security Joyceville. Reid was shunted from prison to prison for a year before landing in Marion, Illinois. After vigorous lobbying, he was transferred in May 1983 to Millhaven, his old haunt.

By that time, Mitchell, too, was back behind bars, serving a twenty-year sentence in the fearsome maximum-security Arizona State Penitentiary. In his book, Weston quotes inmate graffiti to highlight just how fearsome this institution really was: "And on the eighth day, the Lord created Arizona State pen. And He looked down and saw that it was bad. Real bad. And so on the ninth day He created another much better and called it Hell."

Against all odds, Mitchell again demonstrated what a consummate escape artist he was, leaving the prison with two companions via a duct in the roof in May 1986. After fleeing to the Philippines and starting a new life, Mitchell was outed when an acquaintance recognized him on a rerun of Fox's *America's Most Wanted*. In 1994, he was apprehended in Mississippi while on one of his trips back to the States to "visit" banks. Facing decades of prison time, he was shipped off to Leavenworth Penitentiary in Kansas with no hope of parole, and even less of escaping.

///////////////

What has become of the three Stopwatchers in the years since the doors to their respective prison cells clanged definitively shut, finally putting paid to their joint efforts to earn a dishonest living?

Lionel Wright was released in the early 1990s. In 2002, Mitchell noted in his memoir that his old friend was living in Kingston, a stone's throw from the bleak penitentiary. As reported by Josh Dean in *The Atavist Magazine* in 2015, Reid remarked: "One day I noticed Lionel was gone. The letters stopped coming, much in the way that he just vanishes. You don't even know he's gone until someone asks, 'Where's Lionel?' Good question. Where is Lionel?"

Eddie Hertrich provides the answer. Hertrich spent some thirty-five years in Canadian prisons before withdrawing in disgust from his life of crime in 2014 and subsequently writing a gritty memoir called *Wasted Time*. He did time in Millhaven with both Reid and Wright. He says that around 2020, after quietly living and working in Kingston for many years, "The Ghost" passed away from cancer.

According to Paddy Mitchell's sardonic calculations in the epilogue to his book: "My sentence will expire in 2033. I would be in my 91st year then. The judge also tacked on five years supervised release. This would be followed by deportation to Canada to finish off the 14 years I still owe them. I think I'll pass on all of that!"

Little did Mitchell realize how true those words would prove to be.

In 2006, he found a lump under his ribcage. The diagnosis was terminal lung cancer. He desperately petitioned the U.S. authorities to transfer him to Canada, so he could be closer to his son, Kevin, and other family members, but the Americans were having none of it. He got as far as a prison hospital in Butner, North Carolina, where he died alone in January 2007, something he had confessed to a reporter as being his "greatest fear." He was sixty-four.

Stephen Reid was granted a fairytale second chance in life. To counter overwhelming despair while in the "Mill," he poured his feelings into a novel called *Jackrabbit Parole*. The manuscript found its way into the hands of writer and poet Susan Musgrave, who nursed it through to publication. The book was a roaring success. The couple fell in love, married, and had a daughter. On Reid's release from prison in 1987, they moved to Vancouver Island in British Columbia.

Sadly, Reid could not hold things together, lapsing into old, bad, and ruinously expensive habits of cocaine and heroin consumption. In 1999, fuelled by a potent mixture of drugs and desperation, he went back to what (he thought) he knew best — robbing a bank.

A molasses-slow heist at a Royal Bank branch in Victoria resulted in a haul of $93,000, followed by a breakneck police chase through a tourist-filled park, where shots were exchanged, and a standoff in an apartment building. As Dean notes, after more than five hours, the SWAT team moved in. "They found Reid snoring."

Reid was sentenced to eighteen years for the attempted murder of a police officer in pursuit, unlawful confinement, and armed robbery. This spell in prison was different, though. For the first time, with the aid of a prison psychologist, Reid seized the opportunity to confront his demons, and he wrote another book about them. He was paroled in 2014 — and miracle of miracles, his family stood by him. Eventually, he and Musgrave moved to Haida Gwaii.

Reid had survived drug overdoses on several occasions and, in 2009, underwent quintuple bypass surgery. But time was running out for the third and most colourful member of the Stopwatch Gang. The end came in June 2018.

"The day he was admitted to the hospital, seven killer whales came in to the inlet," the CBC quoted Musgrave as saying. "The Haida First Nations belief is that when a killer whale is seen in the inlet, it means that someone is going to die. On Friday there were seven."

Stephen Reid died five days later of what Musgrave described as pulmonary edema and third-degree heart block. He was sixty-eight years old.

9

Fare and Foul

A Christmas Night Escape from the Don Jail

"MURDERER[,] THREE OTHERS FLEE DON JAIL," SCREAMED THE BOLD black headline on the front page of Toronto's *Saturday Star* on December 26, 1981. On Christmas night four men, all described as extremely dangerous, had commandeered a taxi to make their escape.

As twenty-eight-year-old cab driver Leslie Sheppard explained, it was simply a case of being in the wrong place at the wrong time.

Sheppard was working full time as a printer for York Litho and had just purchased a $100,000 house in Pickering, where he was living with his young son. Determined to pay off his mortgage as quickly as possible, he took a second job moonlighting for Diamond Taxi in Toronto. Christmas Day was his first day on the job. He reckoned that spending the holiday away from his family would be a hardship but well worth his while.

He was wrong.

Sheppard had just unloaded a passenger at Riverdale Hospital on Broadview Avenue north of Gerrard Street East, and, in the spirit of Christmas giving, he had escorted the wheelchair-bound patient to the entrance door of the hospital. Returning to his cab, parked on the narrow roadway between the hospital and the red-brick wall of the Toronto (Don) Jail to the south, he began writing up his trip sheet. That was when, as *The Toronto Star* reported on December 27, several men "in the biggest hurry of anyone you ever saw" piled into his taxi. The first guy "was huffing and puffing and said, 'Help us — the bikers are after us. They want to knife us.'" As if to underscore this statement, he noticed that another of the men was shirtless, with a large slash across his chest and stomach. "Go! Go! Go!" they yelled, and he took off, heading west along the laneway, before turning onto Gerrard Street and dropping them off at Sherbourne Street. The fare for the two-to-three-minute ride was $1.70, and he scored a 30-cent tip.

You might think that Sheppard would have made some connection between the four wild-eyed ruffians who jumped into his cab and the notorious jail that loomed just to the south of the roadway where he had parked, but, no — Sheppard professed to be completely gobsmacked to learn, when police stopped him some twelve minutes later, that he had inadvertently helped four desperate criminals to escape from the Don Jail.

An earlier iteration of the Don Jail had stood at the corner of Broadview Avenue and Gerrard Street East since the 1860s. Initially hailed as a veritable "palace for prisoners," with an imposing central administrative block and two wings containing rows of small cells extending to the east and west, the jail soon deteriorated alarmingly. Over the years, it was referred to disparagingly as a "stinking dungeon," a "black hole of Calcutta," or worse. Some of the problems were structural — most of the cells, for example, were minuscule with no toilet facilities, and chronic overcrowding soon became the order of the day.

There are several spectacular escapes from this building on record. In 1919, for example, Frank McCullough, a so-called drifter awaiting execution for the murder of a police officer, wriggled through the bars of the death cell after allegedly doping the night guard. McCullough, soon recaptured, was one of thirty-four men hanged at the jail between 1872 and 1962. And, in the early 1950s, members of the Boyd Gang, a flamboyant band of bank robbers, succeeded, to the extreme mortification of prison authorities, in breaking out — twice!

At the end of 1977, this antiquated jail finally ceased to serve as a correctional institution, and inmates were moved elsewhere.

Many of them ended up in the adjoining east wing, officially called the Toronto Jail, but soon dubbed the New Don, or just the Don. This was a five-storey red-brick Modernist building shaped like a square U, which had been conceived of in the mid-1950s as an addition to the original jail. At the opening ceremony of this new building in November 1958, the jail's governor sounded a warning: while the building had been designed as a maximum-security facility with electronically controlled doors and other security features, he did not consider it escape-proof. "There is always the human element," he told *The Globe and Mail*.

The governor's lack of confidence was more than justified on that December night in 1981, when four inmates confined in the jail's segregation

The corner of Broadview and Victor Avenues, looking west. Taxi driver Leslie Sheppard was parked on the narrow roadway between Riverdale Hospital to the north and the Don Jail to the south when four jailbreakers jumped into his cab.

unit reportedly squeezed through a narrow ventilation shaft, sawed through a steel bar with a hacksaw, and used a rope of blankets and bedsheets spliced together to reach the yard of the old Don Jail. They then scaled a twenty-foot wall to freedom — and that conveniently idling taxicab.

A Canada-wide alert was issued, with Metro Toronto Police out in force. "We are following up every possibility, every tip we have and then going back over them again," a grim Metro police official told the *Star* on December 27. He warned the public not to confront the escapers or "get them upset in any way."

On December 29, an astonishing new development hit the headlines: police had charged the so-called 30-cent-tip cabbie with being an accessory after the fact and assisting in an escape. He was to appear in court early in the new year to have a trial date set.

In the days that followed his ordeal, Sheppard had started to have sober second thoughts about the version of events he had shared with police and the press.

When the four men, uttering dark threats, scrambled into his cab on the roadway between the hospital and the Don Jail, it had in fact taken Sheppard mere moments to realize that his vehicle had been commandeered by a quartet of jailbreakers.

He was ordered to drive along Gerrard Street East and pull over near Parliament Street. He pleaded with the bandits not to steal his cab and gave back the $10 fare one of them had thrust at him. Three of them got out, warning him to keep his mouth shut. The fourth rode for several blocks further and told Sheppard to mislead the police if questioned as to where he had been dropped off.

Sheppard was stopped by police a few minutes later, and he identified himself as the man who had just picked up the foursome outside the jail. It was during the ensuing interview that Sheppard, still trembling from his terrifying encounter, committed the grave error that would plunge him into a year of misery and chaos: he lied. He concocted the story that he had dropped all four men off at Gerrard and Sherbourne Streets, believing that they were being pursued by bikers, and that they had paid $2 for their ride.

Sheppard had dreaded getting involved, and dreaded even more what might happen if the convicts decided to take revenge on him for helping the cops. But over a period of four miserable days, he came to the realization that he had been more than foolish, and he went into a police station to fess up. The police were highly skeptical of his belated efforts to change his story. From their point of view, he was not an innocent victim but someone who had aided the inmates to escape.

Leslie Sheppard's long Christmas nightmare had begun.

////////////////////

Ranked from bad to worst, the four criminals who escaped from the Don Jail on Christmas night were Randolph "Randy" Garrison, Brian William Bush, Andre Hirsh, and Terrance "Terry" Derek Musgrave. All of them were in their twenties. All had conducted their criminal activities in Toronto or neighbouring cities like North York (not part of the city of Toronto at the time), and their combined rap sheets contained more than eighty offences.

Randy Garrison of Toronto had received a three-year prison sentence for robbing a Kingston Road service station in 1979 and was facing a further trial at the time on charges of robbery and assault causing bodily harm.

Scarborough native Brian Bush was awaiting trial on charges of armed robbery and possession of a restricted weapon. Bush's claim to fame — or infamy — was his membership of the Dirty Tricks Gang, so-called because of the creative diversionary tactics they adopted while carrying out their heists. Their preferred modus operandi when making a getaway by car was to scatter planks or lengths of hose studded with nails on the roadway to puncture the tires of pursuing vehicles. In March 1981, Bush had been involved in an abortive robbery at a Royal Bank branch in Leaside. Metro Toronto Police had received a "vague tip" that something might be going down, and they were waiting outside the bank when the masked bandits fled with their haul of around $24,000. In the firefight that ensued, police shot one of the robbers dead and wounded two others. Bush was arrested in Yorkville after a high-speed car chase through the city.

Andre Hirsh of Toronto was awaiting trial on a charge of first-degree murder after a bungled holdup at a Weston Road jewellery store in May 1981. When confronted at gunpoint during the robbery, the store owner, thirty-eight-year-old Frank Abrams, had flatly refused to hand over any money or jewellery. He was shot outside his store while trying to wrest the firearm from his attacker. As Hirsh attempted to flee, a group of bystanders brought him down. As the *Star* reported sombrely in October 1982, Hirsh told police that Abrams "had it coming to him," adding, "the guy had to play Joe Hero." Abrams had threatened to fetch his dogs, "so I unloaded on him ... not in the head or heart but in the stomach." The truth was starkly different: Abrams was shot three times, including once through the heart.

And at the top (or bottom) spot, at very worst, was self-confessed murderer Terry Musgrave of North York. His brutal crime had horrified the city back in January 1981. The victim was Catherine Maruya, the forty-three-year-old owner of a ceramic studio in North York, who was found bound and gagged at her workplace. She had been stabbed twenty-eight times with a pair of scissors and strangled. Musgrave, described by the prosecutor at his trial as "a cold-blooded killer," had pleaded guilty to second-degree murder. He had received an automatic life sentence and was being held at the Don pending the judge's decision as to the minimum time he would serve.

As per the *Star* on December 31, 1981, a representative of the Don Jail's 145 full-time and twenty-four part-time guards told the press bluntly that "the escape came as no surprise to us at all." One of the problems was the location of the segregation unit, which guards could not easily monitor. But the most pressing concern was chronic overcrowding — an average in the facility of between 440 and 460 inmates a day, well above the maximum of 319 prescribed by Ontario's correctional ministry. "If there were fewer prisoners in the jail, prisoners in segregation could be moved to a safer area," added the spokesman.

Musgrave, unquestionably the baddest of the jailbreaking bunch, was the first to be picked up by Metro police. He was spotted by two uniformed officers outside a shopping plaza on Jane Street in North York and arrested at gunpoint.

Handcuffed and in shackles, Musgrave appeared in court at College Park in Toronto on December 29. His charges, as might be presumed, were serious: escaping custody and possession of a prohibited firearm — a sawed-off .22-calibre rifle. He was eager to get things over with. ("I don't want a lawyer. I plead guilty," the *Star* of December 30 quoted him as saying.) At the judge's insistence, he agreed to have his case remanded for a week — both to consult a lawyer and to get treatment for a foot fracture. He had broken a bone when jumping over the jail wall.

The second fugitive to be corralled was Randy Garrison, who surrendered on December 28, after just three days on the lam. Garrison had telephoned his father, Ernest, asking him to arrange for two officers to meet him at a street light on the corner of Driftwood and Finch Avenues in North York.

The following day, Sergeant Don Bell and Constable Steve McAteer told the *Star* that they duly "went and stood there." And, in true noir fashion, "Garrison just appeared out of the darkness."

Garrison was exhausted. Since his escape, he had managed to snatch just a couple of hours' sleep each night. He was also terrified, after reading newspaper reports that he was regarded as a suspect in a robbery at a York borough gas station the day before. Three bandits in ski-masks had bound and gagged the attendant and threatened him with a knife. Garrison later swore to both the police and his father that he had played no part in that robbery. His overriding fear was that the longer he stayed on the run, the more he would be blamed for any crimes committed in the future. The police believed his story.

The police also believed that he had nothing to do with planning the jailbreak.

Garrison was "the odd man out," said Sergeant Bell. "We felt he would be the one who would give himself up."

At Garrison's trial on January 26, 1982, as recorded in the next day's *Star*, Bell told the court that the hapless inmate first learned of the "elaborate escape plan" on Christmas Day, when he was transferred to that segregated (and poorly supervised) area on the second floor of the Don where Musgrave, Hirsh, and Bush were already sequestered. When his three fellow escapees piled into the taxi after the escape, Garrison tried to run away. But the vehicle drew up beside him and someone called out: "Randy, get in." As evidence of Garrison's reluctance, Bell testified that police had found a note on his person written on the back of a cigarette box. It read: "I Terry Musgrave forced Randy Garrison to go with us." Musgrave later confirmed that he had written it.

Garrison, who pleaded guilty to being "at large," was sentenced to three months in jail, to be added to the three years he was already serving for the gas station robbery in 1979.

Terry Musgrave and Randy Garrison, both back inside.

And then there were two …

On January 3, 1982, by pure accident, the third fugitive was located and escorted back into the fold.

That Sunday, the Ontario Provincial Police (OPP) detachment at Lindsay received a tip from a sharp-eyed cottager in Kenrei Park, a small community around five kilometres north of Lindsay, that someone appeared to be occupying a cottage that should, rightly, have been unoccupied. Three officers paid a visit to the community to check things out; there was indeed a trespasser. After surrounding the cottage, they took the intruder into custody. The man was alone and unarmed, and he offered no resistance.

It was only after the arrest that the OPP established his identity — Brian William Bush, who had been charged with robbery and possessing restricted weapons. Metro Toronto Police had earlier described Bush as very dangerous. Their Lindsay counterparts must have thanked their lucky stars that he had had none of those lethal weapons on his person at the time.

On February 9, Bush was convicted for his part in the bungled Leaside bank robbery in March 1981 that had left one of his fellow bandits dead and two others wounded in a shootout with police. This was his third robbery conviction. As reported in the *Star* the day after his trial, a stern Judge Hugh Locke told the court that Bush regarded "jail as an occupational hazard. He knew there were weapons being used. He is a very dangerous man with dire prospects for rehabilitation." He sentenced Bush to eleven years in prison.

Of the four malefactors, Andre Hirsh was now the last man (out)-standing.

FARE AND FOUL

That changed on September 24, 1982, when Staff Sergeant Julian Fantino and Sergeant Robert Montrose of Metro Toronto Police flew to Los Angeles. This was no pleasure trip — their purpose was to pick up two fugitive murder suspects and escort them back to Toronto. The first of these was Robert Palmer, who had allegedly bludgeoned his father to death with a hammer. The second was Andre Hirsh, being extradited on the orders of a U.S. federal judge. Hirsh had fled down south after his escape from the Don.

On October 22, 1982, the *Star* gave a detailed account of Fantino's testimony at Hirsh's trial. When taken into custody after the botched robbery, Hirsh had described himself as "the black sheep" of his family. He was heavily indebted to loan sharks and "had to have the bread [cash] … or else." The court heard about Hirsh's struggle with Abrams outside the store, when Hirsh had shot the jeweller three times, one bullet piercing his heart.

Crown Counsel Chris Rutherford was appalled at the "cold-blooded killing." As reported in *The Globe and Mail* on December 1, 1982, he declared that Hirsh "should be locked up and locked up for a long time.… He killed an innocent, peaceable shopkeeper who had the absolute audacity to stand up for his property."

Also on December 1, in an article titled "Killer Gets Life, Tells Widow He's 'Sorry,'" the *Star* published a full report of Hirsh's final court appearance, which had taken place on November 30.

Hirsh was found guilty of second-degree murder. Before his sentence was handed down, his defence lawyer read to the court a one-page handwritten letter of apology, addressed to Frank Abrams's widow. Part of it stated: "I am not a cold-blooded vicious person without conscience.… I feel the disgust you must have for me; it shames me strongly. Please understand that there is no limit to the remorse I feel and will carry with me forever.… I'm sorry, I'm truly sorry."

Hirsh's letter failed to alter the opinion of Mr. Justice John O'Driscoll. "There may be some degree of remorse in you," he told Hirsh. But "you are also more than somewhat of a con man." He sentenced Hirsh to life imprisonment with no parole for at least sixteen years.

On Tuesday, December 21, 1982, after a series of ten abortive court appearances due to ongoing congestion within the system, Leslie Sheppard finally had his moment of truth before a York County Court judge. Sheppard faced a two-to-three-year prison sentence for being an accessory after the fact to the escape of the four felons on December 25, 1981.

On December 23, the *Star*'s Ellie Tesher gave readers the full scoop on the *annus horribilis* of the erstwhile taxi driver.

In the course of the twelve months since he had committed the cardinal sin of lying to the police, Sheppard had been overwhelmed both financially and emotionally. He'd had to sell his house to cover the thousands of dollars he spent on legal fees. He was depressed, fearful of going out, and terrified that, in spite of being innocent, he would be sent to jail.

His lawyer, Eddie Greenspan, called him "the ultimate victim of circumstances — this poor sap who walked into an utter horror story."

On Tuesday, December 21, 1982, the judge agreed with Greenspan. His client was acquitted of all charges.

And a delighted Sheppard told Tesher, "Now I believe in Christmas again."

10

There Be Monsters

Allan Legere, Harvey Andres, and the Emergence of Forensic DNA Profiling

FOR ANYONE WONDERING WHAT THE MIRAMICHI RIVER VALLEY IS famous for, the definitive answer from Tourism New Brunswick is "salmon fishing and local friendliness." Its website invites you to delve into the region's history, with its abundant ghost stories, lumberjack legends, and local folklore.

In the last three decades of the twentieth century, however, a much grimmer narrative seared itself into the public's consciousness in the Miramichi — the saga of Allan Joseph Legere.

According to a *Globe and Mail* report by Robert Jones in November 1989, Legere, born in 1948 in Chatham Head, New Brunswick, was exceptionally well-known to police while still in his teens. He was nicknamed "the bad boy" by locals, who endured years of beatings and burglaries at his hands. His first conviction as an adult was an eighteen-month sentence for theft in 1967. After that, arrests and convictions came in thick and fast: assault, possession of stolen property, breaking and entering, dangerous driving, possession of a dangerous weapon, resisting arrest.

He fell under suspicion for the 1974 murder of a Newcastle woman, Mary Beatrice Redmond. She was stabbed more than eighty times after returning home from Saturday night mass in nearby Chatham Head, but the frustrated police could not find sufficient evidence to lay charges. According to Newcastle Deputy Police Chief Jack White, however, that was when people became really afraid.

Legere added to his nefarious accomplishments by becoming a cat burglar in the 1980s, with a razor as his weapon of choice. According to one oft-repeated story, he allegedly cut the underwear off a woman during a nighttime robbery in Moncton — without waking her.

On June 21, 1986, Legere committed an atrocious crime at Black River Bridge, just outside Newcastle. He broke into the home of storekeeper John Glendenning with two accomplices in tow, demanding the combination of Glendenning's safe. The sixty-six-year-old man was bound, viciously beaten, and choked to death with a shirt knotted round his neck. His wife, Mary, sixty-two, was sexually assaulted, beaten unconscious, strangled with a pair of nylon stockings, and left for dead. The thieves made off with $25,000, which was not recovered.

Against all odds, Mary Glendenning lived to testify at the trial of the three killers in Newcastle in early 1987. Legere's co-accused surprised the court by changing their pleas to guilty just before the widow took the stand. Despite his protestations of innocence, Legere was described by the Crown as the main perpetrator of the "brutal, gruesome, senseless crime." He was convicted of second-degree murder and sentenced to life in prison with no chance of parole for eighteen years.

For twenty-eight months, sequestered at the Atlantic Institution, a maximum-security penitentiary at Renous, New Brunswick, Legere was a model inmate, toeing the line and fostering good relations with prison staff. So, when he complained of an ear infection on May 3, 1989, and was escorted by two unarmed guards to the Dr. Georges-L.-Dumont Regional Hospital in Moncton for treatment, his chaperones had no qualms about allowing this pleasant, compliant prisoner to go to the toilet alone. After all, he was wearing handcuffs and leg shackles at the time.

What could possibly go wrong?

They were probably more than a little shocked when Legere burst out of the washroom sans cuffs and shackles, threatened them with a pointed tool that he had secreted in his rectum — he also had a cigar containing a piece of metal that he had used to cut off his restraints — and ran out of the hospital. He hijacked a car, taking the driver, a woman named Peggy Olive, hostage. She was released unharmed.

Too late, Atlantic Institution warden Don Wheaton came to recognize what he referred to in a *Globe and Mail* piece in November as Legere's "Jekyll-and-Hyde personality."

The man who became known as the Monster of the Miramichi was on the prowl.

Ominously, police revealed that Legere had vowed to wreak vengeance on local residents. Three and a half weeks after his escape, the vicious assaults and killings began.

The victims included Annie Flam, an elderly shopkeeper in Newcastle who was beaten to death before her house was set on fire; her sister-in-law, Nina Flam, who was left battered but alive in their burning home; sisters Donna and Linda Daughney, whose bodies were found by firefighters battling a blaze in their Newcastle home; and Father James Smith, a Chatham Head priest who was bludgeoned to death in his rectory.

After the Daughney slayings, amid bitter complaints that the RCMP wasn't doing enough to protect the public, the manhunt intensified, and the Canadian Crime Stoppers Association offered a reward of $10,000 for information leading to Legere's arrest. Eventually, the reward would be raised to $50,000.

In a "Letter from Newcastle" published in the *Globe* on November 4, 1989, Rick MacLean, editor of *The Miramichi Leader*, sketched a chilling picture of a tiny community, completely traumatized. "This is small-town New Brunswick. Chatham and Newcastle [both absorbed into the city of

Miramichi in 1995] are 10 kilometres apart and have about 6,000 people in each. There are about 20,000 people in the immediate area. We're not used to this kind of thing." People who had never before locked their doors were locking them now; buying extra lighting, phones, and alarm systems; and, despite police warnings, keeping loaded guns in their homes. Senior citizens were afraid to remain in their houses, and Halloween festivities had been cancelled.

According to a chronology of events in the University of New Brunswick's Allan Legere Digital Archive, on the night of November 23, 1989, with snow falling heavily and ice building up on the roads, Ron Gomke, a taxi driver in Saint John, picked up a man who wanted a ride to Moncton, some 180 kilometres away.

"We're going to Moncton," said the man, waving a sawed-off .308 rifle for emphasis. "I'm Allan Legere."

The driver struggled in vain to keep the car on the icy road; shortly after leaving Moncton, it spun out of control and plowed into a snowbank.

Forcing Gomke out of the taxi, Legere flagged down a passing car, driven by Michelle Mercer, an off-duty RCMP officer from Montreal. The two men piled in. Legere again produced his gun and insisted that they proceed to Moncton. About halfway there, Mercer had to pull in to a small gas station to refuel. After filling up, Legere took the car keys and went into the store to pay.

Left in the car, Mercer and Gomke had a short, tense conversation. Mercer had a spare set of keys and thought they should make a run for it.

"Will he let us go?" asked Gomke.

"No," replied Mercer.

"Then we have nothing to lose," said Gomke, and they drove off.

By the time they reached a nearby RCMP control centre and sounded the alarm, sending police speeding to the gas station, Legere was gone. He had hijacked a tractor-trailer, forcing the driver to carry on toward Moncton, then Newcastle.

But the net was closing fast.

An RCMP team had pinpointed his whereabouts, and, shortly after 5:00 a.m. on November 24, they were able to radio in the welcome news that they had succeeded in taking Legere into custody. Without a struggle.

In a short piece entitled "Allan Legere: A Look Back," journalist and author André Veniot recalls his impressions of the day of Legere's capture: "How the sun shone... and how absolutely delighted and happy people were. A weight, a huge weight had been lifted off their shoulders. That first sight of Allan Legere, thin, no beard, being escorted from the RCMP detachment while hundreds of people watched. The party at the Wharf Inn afterwards."

Legere was considered a suspect in all four killings. However, the case against him was purely circumstantial. There were no eyewitnesses, and evidence-gathering had been compromised by the fact that the homes of several victims had been destroyed by fire.

But police and prosecutors had a significant, state-of-the-art card up their sleeves. They played it to great effect in late 1991 during Legere's trial in Burton, New Brunswick, on four first-degree murder charges.

Front and centre in the courtroom were specialists in the field of deoxyribonucleic acid (DNA) profiling, who had compared blood taken from a tissue discarded by Legere on the day of his recapture to semen found at the crime scenes. The challenge, as noted by Crown prosecutor John J. Walsh, QC, was that this technique was regarded at the time as "novel scientific evidence."

Would cutting-edge DNA evidence be admissible to the court?

For the first time in a major Canadian case, the answer was yes.

The jury accepted the testimony of the Crown's experts, who stated that the possibility of the semen found on the body of Nina Flam belonging to anyone *other* than Legere was as high as 5.2 million to one. The odds were as high as 310 million to one in the case of Linda Daughney. Taking the genetic evidence into account along with the circumstantial evidence presented during the trial, the eleven-person jury had no hesitation in returning a verdict of guilty on all four counts of first-degree murder.

Legere was declared a dangerous offender — a designation "earned" only by the most violent Canadian criminals — and sent to the ultra-high or supermax security Special Handling Unit (SHU) within the federal Regional Reception Centre at Sainte-Anne-des-Plaines, near Montreal.

Harrowing memories of the Miramichi "reign of terror" came flooding back in 2015, when it was announced that Legere had been transferred from

York County Jail in Fredericton, New Brunswick, where serial killer Allan Legere was imprisoned in 1991 during his trial on four counts of first-degree murder.

the SHU to a regular maximum-security facility, the Edmonton Institution in Alberta.

"He could escape any institution, I think, if the opportunity comes along, and I'm sure for the last twenty-five years that's where his mind has been all the time, trying to connive and think of some way that if he ever gets the opportunity how he would go about doing it," dismayed Miramichi deputy mayor John Foran told the CBC.

////////////////

Edmonton Institution (or Max) is a federal prison built in 1978 to house 324 inmates on eighteen acres of land at a cost of $15.2 million. From the outset, Edmonton Max boasted extensive security features: double chain-link fences topped with razor wire; microwave motion detectors between the fences; armed guards in lookout towers; and video surveillance throughout.

However, despite being labelled "escape proof," the facility saw three well-publicized escapes in the first few years of its existence; notably, two by the same individual — Harvey Harold Andres.

Born in 1948 and described as "tall, muscular, and mean," Andres, a former member of the Alberta-based Grim Reapers outlaw motorcycle gang, was serving a twenty-five-year sentence for the first-degree murder of Shirley Ann Baker, raped and beaten to death in her Winfield, British Columbia, home in 1976. Prior to that, Andres's rap sheet had included sixty convictions for breaking and entering and robbery, dating back to his pre-teen years.

For two years, Andres kept to himself in the prison, quietly focusing on painting, metalwork, and weightlifting. Then, on March 12, 1981, he placed a hand-painted dummy in his bed and literally went out with the trash: he crawled into a metal garbage container behind the jail. He was tipped into a compactor truck and driven to the dump, saving himself from being crushed by using a wooden beam as a brace.

His freedom lasted forty days. He was brought down in a hail of bullets in Calgary while trying to flee from the police in a Ford Pinto. One of the bullets went through the trunk of the car, penetrated the back seat and the driver's seat, and lodged near his kidney. An RCMP officer was also shot, embarrassingly struck by a bullet from the gun of a city police officer.

Andres's second escape from Edmonton Max on March 11, 1982 — that is, just one year after the first — was perhaps even more audacious.

The Vancouver Sun edition of March 25 called it "strictly a snow job."

While some guards "vainly squinted" at video monitors and others "skidded around snow-clogged grounds in the worst blizzard of the winter," Andres and four fellow cons coolly made their escape — all dressed in long underwear, white clothes filched from the kitchen, and white bedsheets. They possibly got out by unlocking a door leading to the centre courtyard. After climbing up and over the cell block, Andres et al. used wire cutters (conveniently "lost" by an electrician a couple of weeks earlier) to clip through the two six-metre-high chain-link perimeter fences.

At this point, the paths of the escapees diverged. With alarms blaring and lights flashing, armed prison guards who had scrambled into two jeeps raced to the break in the fence. They were just in time to nab Andres's four accomplices.

The probable ringleader, however, had vanished into the storm.

It took police 117 days to nail Andres, this time in Saskatoon. On July 6, armed and wearing a wig and dark glasses, he broke into a home on the hunt for cash, taking the occupants hostage. Neighbours who had seen a stranger enter the house alerted the police. After an exchange of gunfire, Andres bolted and was finally shot down at a nearby strip mall. In spite of having gravely wounded him, police still had to wrestle the burly man to the ground to cuff him.

///////////////////

In 2015, the worried citizens of Miramichi voiced their fears that Allan Legere might find a way to escape from a possibly less-secure prison in Alberta and return to New Brunswick to once again cause havoc in his old haunts. Paying no heed to their pleas, the powers that be refused to reverse their decision to transfer the killer to Edmonton Max.

Granted, Legere would not have too comfortable a stay in Edmonton. For years, according to correctional investigator Ivan Zinger in his 2018–19 Annual Report: "Edmonton Institution … has been plagued by a toxic and troubled workplace culture where dysfunction, abuse of power, and harassment have festered."

With regard to escapes, though, Chris Nelson of *The Calgary Herald* noted reassuringly in 2013 that "this isn't 1982, when Harvey Andres escaped under the fence [sic] in a snowstorm … things are tighter at the pen these days."

Just as well.

During the four months that Andres was on the loose after his escape in 1982, the city of Calgary had become the nexus of a terrifying crime spree. Between April 26 and June 3, seven women were raped by a man described as wearing a ski mask and armed with a handgun.

On May 23, 1982, police made a grim discovery: the lifeless body of seventeen-year-old Shirley Ann Johnston in a broom closet locked from the outside in her burned-out Calgary home. Johnston had been sexually assaulted, and the fire had been deliberately set.

Her boyfriend, Kelly Wilson, admitted that he had had consensual sex with her but hotly denied that he had harmed her in any way. He said that he had left her house around 12:30 a.m. Arson investigators determined that the fire must have started after 4:00 a.m. As he was the last person known to have seen Johnston alive, Wilson was regarded as a suspect, but charges were never laid.

Regarding the rash of sexual assaults, a special investigative team and the Calgary police sex crimes unit came to the conclusion that all seven women were abused by the same person. Here, Andres was the prime and immediate suspect. This line of investigation seemed to fizzle out, however. According to a January 1983 headline in *The Calgary Herald*, "Special squad clears Harvey Andres of unsolved rapes."

But Calgary police held onto the evidence, including vaginal swabs taken from Johnston's body during her autopsy — although there was not much they could do with it at the time.

Flash forward to 1997, when the Calgary detective who had handled the case retired and handed the files over to his successor.

With a new team on the case and DNA analysis now well established as a forensic tool, the criminal investigation was revived in earnest. A DNA warrant was finally obtained from a judge in February 1999, authorizing police to take a blood sample from Harvey Andres, who was still serving a life sentence in Edmonton Max for the 1976 murder of Shirley Ann Baker.

"It took quite a while but we had to wait for DNA technology to catch up," commented the lead investigator, Detective Robin Greenwood, in the November 3, 2001, edition of *The Calgary Herald*.

Nineteen years after the brutal rapes of at least five women and the murder of another, justice was finally done. On November 3, 2001, Andres was found guilty of first-degree murder and arson. Sentencing him to a second automatic life sentence without parole for twenty-five years, the stern judge stated that he had no doubt that Andres had raped and callously confined Johnston without possibility of escape before setting fire to her house, leaving her to die of carbon monoxide poisoning.

Allan Legere and Harvey Andres have in common that they have both done time at the redoubtable Edmonton Institution. There are other striking similarities. Both men are serving life sentences as gratuitously violent sex criminals and ruthless killers. In addition, a novel scientific breakthrough, DNA profiling, was the vital factor that sank Allan Legere in 1991. And, in an ironic twist of fate some ten years later, DNA analysis, now an essential part of the forensic investigation tool kit, would be used to solve a nagging cold case, finally bringing Harvey Andres to justice.

11

Porous Walls

Oakalla Prison Farm: "A Punishing Yet Easily Escapable Institution"

IN 1911, THE RESIDENTS OF BURNABY, BRITISH COLUMBIA, WERE incensed to learn that provincial plans were afoot to construct a prison farm on 185 acres of pristine, wooded land overlooking Deer Lake, with gorgeous vistas of the North Shore Mountains. They were not placated by a report, quoted in *Corrections in British Columbia: Pre-Confederation to the Millennium*, that "the new central prison is to be both structurally and in equipment thoroughly up-to-date, having been carefully planned with a view to obtaining perfect light, ventilation and sanitation, in conjunction with absolute security."

In support, the Burnaby Board of Trade forwarded "a respectful protest to the provincial government against the establishment of a prison farm on

D.L. 84, in the midst of the best residential locality in Burnaby," which would require "the occupation of a site worth in the market over $300,000, while the government possesses other lands, 160 acres in extent, in Burnaby, worth only $95,000." For comparison, that would be about $8 million and $2.5 million in today's dollars, respectively.

The provincial authorities were in a bind. They saw the New Westminster Gaol, the nineteenth-century relic that currently served the lower British Columbian mainland, as irredeemable — mouldering, chronically overcrowded, and dangerously insecure. They envisioned a working prison farm with its own dairy, vegetable gardens, and farm animals that would house — and employ — around 480 male and female offenders either sentenced to terms of two years less one day or awaiting trial, appeal, or transfer to a federal penitentiary.

Therefore, the Burnaby BoT's respectful protest was ignored, and in 1912 the first batch of male inmates arrived at the new facility, officially named Oakalla Prison Farm — Oakalla for short — and, eventually, the Lower Mainland Regional Correctional Centre. A section for women opened in 1916.

Like Kingston Penitentiary, which dated back to 1833 and became the model for the Canadian penitentiary system for upward of a century, Oakalla, a four-wing red-brick structure, was based on the Auburn system of penology — strict discipline with hard work in total silence for inmates during the day and solitary confinement at night.

The original promise of "absolute security" soon proved to be hollow.

In his book *Hard Place to Do Time*, Earl Andersen, who worked in the 1980s as a correctional officer at Oakalla, describes the place as "a punishing yet easily escapable institution." This was, if anything, a gross understatement. There was no problem at all in filling, or overfilling, the cells at Oakalla, but when it came to actually *keeping* inmates inside, Oakalla was an epic fail. Between 1940 and 1990 alone, according to statistics quoted by Andersen, more than 890 men, women, and young offenders succeeded in escaping.

Each successive decade brought its own litany of crises and calamities.

For example, in August 1926 armed guards supervising a work gang in a hay field at the northern edge of the prison grounds yelled at two inmates

The main block of Oakalla Prison Farm, renamed the Lower Mainland Regional Correctional Centre in 1970.

for talking on the job, which was strictly forbidden at the time. The two men, William Lane, eighteen years old, and twenty-two-year-old William Brewster seemed to comply; then, suddenly, they took off, heading for the fence — exceptionally speedily, given their work clothes and heavy boots. After the fugitives had ignored several warnings to stop, the officers let fly a volley of bullets in their direction. Twelve shots were fired; one of the bullets hit Brewster in the back, tearing through his chest. His companion threw his hands up and surrendered. Brewster was rushed by ambulance to the Vancouver General Hospital, where he was pronounced dead on arrival.

That was the only time an inmate would be shot to death by a guard at Oakalla. But it was not the first time, nor, chillingly, would it be the last, that blood would flow in this grim place.

In March 1931, there was another death, this one in the public eye.

Two inmates, both in their twenties, were being held at Oakalla pending sentencing on several counts of armed robbery. Ellis Wilcox and Fraser McDougall, the latter described by victims as "the grinning bandit," knew that they would probably end up having to serve some twenty years in the extremely well-guarded British Columbia Penitentiary at New Westminster.

Their best chance for a successful getaway would be from leaky Oakalla. After their return from a court session, they seized the opportunity to escape from the front hall of the main building by overpowering the guards, using weapons slipped to them by an associate.

After several clashes with the public and police over the next few days, the fugitives were confronted in Burnaby by four officers, including Chief Constable William Devitt of the Burnaby Police Department, who prided himself on being an expert marksman.

The chief called on them to surrender, but, as he told *The Vancouver Sun* on March 14, Wilcox suddenly "pulled out two revolvers and started to fire. I heard the bullets singing over my head; but, in the excitement, I could not say how many shots he fired. And then I let him have it."

Wilcox died almost instantaneously. The rifle shot severed his finger, bounced off one of his guns, and pierced his abdomen. After trading gunfire with the police, McDougall finally capitulated and was taken back to Oakalla.

Possibly the most outrageous escape of all took place in April 1937. One of the escapees was Vernon "Blackie" Campbell, aged twenty-five; the other, twenty-seven-year-old Gordon Fawcett, was awaiting trial on charges of auto theft, unlawful possession of a weapon, and attempted murder. He was already a seasoned jailbreaker, after escaping from Oakalla with four other bandits in early 1932 and spending two months on the run before being recaptured.

Like a number of local and provincially run penal institutions throughout Canada — among them Toronto's first (and exceptionally notorious) Don Jail — Oakalla was a hanging jail. Between the years of 1919 and 1959, forty-four inmates met their end at Oakalla at the end of a rope. Initially, executions were held outdoors, but in 1931 a small room on the second floor of the south wing was converted into an execution chamber, with the gallows positioned above a trap door in the floor.

Fawcett and Campbell gained entrance to the gallows chamber through two locked doors. The fact that the doors were then locked behind them from the outside strongly suggests the collaboration of a fellow inmate, or even, perhaps, a guard.

Because the chamber served as a storeroom between hangings, it was conveniently piled high with sheets and blankets. After sawing through the bars in the outer window, the men used the bedding to form a rope, lowered themselves to the ground, and fled.

Campbell made it to Washington State. A month after the escape, he died in a hospital in Tacoma following a bungled robbery and a shootout with police. Fawcett resurfaced in 1941. After being arrested in California, he served a prison term of eighteen months and was then sent back to Oakalla.

By the 1940s, special training and other privileges had been put in place for young male first offenders. Referred to as the "Gazoonie Gang" and later the "Star Class," they were housed in two tiers or levels separate from the general prison population. Clearly underwhelmed by official efforts on their behalf, fourteen of them, aged between fifteen and twenty-one, sawed through the bars and took off in a mass escape at the end of November 1947 — the largest ever at Oakalla, although others came close. After what Andersen calls "a small crime-wave" in the area, police started reeling in the escapees.

Within two days, half of them were back in custody. Three of the fugitives stole an unmarked police cruiser in Vancouver and crossed into the U.S. They were at large for four days before being picked up in Oregon, one of them carrying a loaded .25-calibre automatic weapon. By December 9, all of the runaways were safely back under lock and key.

Although two guards were fired for negligence and security was increased in the tiers, the warden of the day flatly refused to have the youngsters locked down during mealtimes. On New Year's Day, 1949, another eight Star Class delinquents made the most of this leniency — taking their cue from the class of '47, they sawed through the bars and scampered away. Shortly thereafter, five of them were found hanging out at the nearby Industrial School for Girls, puffing on stolen cigarettes.

In 1948, after complaining bitterly about the food (quoted by Andersen as "generally cold with a film of grease on top of it") and living conditions (including allegations of lice in the bedding), sixty inmates went on a rampage, smashing thirty windows in the process. The window-breakers were punished with up to ten paddle strokes — a whipping across the bare backside with a leather strap — and, in protest, inmates went on a food strike.

Following this riot, public pressure forced the province to launch a commission of inquiry. One of the findings, to no one's surprise, was that Oakalla was massively overcrowded. In 1950, for example, the prison population was at eight hundred and counting. By 1952, it had exceeded nine hundred.

Despite attempts by Warden Hugh Christie to improve conditions and introduce rehabilitation programs at Oakalla, dissatisfaction continued to bubble up to the surface. In October 1952, amid a tangle of shattered glass and broken furniture, and to a chorus of howling men and women protesting against overcrowding, about a hundred rioting inmates took two guards hostage in the south wing of the jail.

One of the guards found his rescue more harrowing than his three hours of captivity. Reportedly "haggard and still visibly nervous," he told *The Ottawa Citizen* on October 3: "The tear gas was sure grim. I was soaked from head to foot with water and tears were pouring out of my eyes when the rest of the guards got to me."

The year 1955 was particularly fraught. One of the first events was a cheeky (and embarrassing) escape in March. William Babcock, described as "a menace to society" with a record of forty-eight convictions including armed robbery, quietly mingled with a visiting choir and strolled away after a Sunday church service. He was found two months later on a stolen fishing boat, headed for Alaska. Shock and horror greeted reports of a grotesque incident in June: a violent hanging that saw the condemned man verbally and physically attack the hangman before being dragged to the gallows. In November, four inmates, all with long sentences, made a run for it from the exercise yard. After a vicious exchange of gunfire with the guards at the gate, they commandeered a car and escaped into a wooded area nearby. Although they were all caught within a couple of days, the publicity around their escape and the massive manhunt that followed led to renewed demands by local residents for the prison to be relocated.

By the 1960s, with the prison population hovering around the twelve-hundred mark, the bricks and mortar of the fifty-year-old jail were crumbling — a fact that was emphasized in 1963 when two inmates on the top floor of the west wing made their escape by hacking a two-foot-wide hole through the concrete ceiling of their cell and the roof above it.

The west wing was again the scene of trouble in 1964, when a drug addict complained to fellow inmates that the medical officer had refused him withdrawal medication. Officials succeeded in preventing a riot then, but, the following morning, the concerns of another inmate, described as "a perpetual complainer," were not followed up promptly enough, and the man hanged himself in his cell. That night, all hell broke loose. Andersen quotes the warden of the day as saying that staff members kept "patrolling all tiers constantly ... without flinching, ... walking over piles of debris and wading through water from burst plumbing lines and fire hoses." The disturbance racked up more than $30,000 in damages.

During the 1960s, suicides spiked at Oakalla, as evidenced by this shocking extract in *Hard Place to Do Time* from the 1964–65 annual report of the senior medical officer: "There has been a marked increase in pathological behaviour within the gaol. This has taken the form of 5 suicides and 57 attempted suicides, of which 27 were slashing, 17 were attempted hangings, 10 were by swallowing metal (spoons, etc.) 2 swallowing toxic substances, and 1 attempted drowning."

As if hundreds of breakouts from the prison were not sufficiently deplorable, in July 1970 Oakalla had the distinction of being the scene of a well-publicized break-*in*. A radical group in Vancouver calling itself the Youth International Party, whose members were known as Yippies, declared that it was planning a "Be-Out" just outside the prison grounds as a protest against the vile conditions within. Toward evening, about three hundred Yippies managed to tear down a section of the perimeter fence, and a few brave souls ventured onto the grounds. Faced with around eighty guards in riot gear and a sizable contingent of RCMP officers, the main bunch contented themselves with yelling obscenities before sensibly retiring to a nearby park for an evening of speeches, music, and frisbee throwing.

In October 1979, after spending two days in Oakalla (by now called the Lower Mainland Regional Correctional Centre) at the invitation of correctional officials, Judge Cunliffe Barnett was quoted in the *Vancouver Sun* as describing the institution as a "cold, hostile environment," adding that it was "hopelessly outdated, old, patched up and not clean, and your first impression is that a lot of good people are trying hard under terrible circumstances to do the best job they can."

Those conditions would rapidly deteriorate even further, putting both inmates and staff at risk.

After several women's riots in the 1970s, a full-blown, thirteen-hour disturbance took place on New Year's Eve in 1980. This ushered in a wave of violence that lasted two months, with the women bitterly alleging that guards were abusing them.

The worst riot of all took place in November 1983. Tensions caused by the juxtaposition of sentenced inmates and those on remand (awaiting trial) in the west wing exploded into an after-dinner rampage. More than one hundred rowdies were involved, setting fire to cells, smashing furniture and plumbing fixtures, and, ominously, threatening to seize a guard. Using pieces of pipe and other ad hoc implements, they hacked at and broke through an outer wall. Staff deployed fire hoses to put out blazes and dampen the fury of the mob; it took until midnight, however, before the riot finally subsided. The following morning, the media was invited in to survey the chaos at what *The Montreal Gazette* ironically called the "sometimes-unruly provincial jail." Damage was assessed at around $150,000. That would be approximately $430,000 today.

Then came the events of December 1987 and January 1988.

On December 11, three inmates made their escape during a recreation period by cutting a hole through an outer wall and climbing over a perimeter fence. They allegedly left the area by public transit, still wearing their prison garb. This event, which went undetected for some hours, was only brought to general attention in early January. As *The Globe and Mail* pointed out on January 5, 1988, an RCMP spokesman would offer no explanation as to why the break was not disclosed until nearly a month after it took place. "On occasion prisoners get out," he said.

But the defining episode in Oakalla's long and violent history would start innocuously enough on December 27, 1987, when a man was expelled from chapel for allegedly talking during church services. In a scuffle with guards, he received a cut over his eye that required stitches. Reaction to the incident spread like wildfire, leading to a riot in the south wing. The following day, the inmates were locked down and unrest flared up again. Inmates accused the guards of spraying them with water from high-pressure hoses, which left them drenched and cold and damaged their possessions. Windows were opened, ostensibly to clear the smoke from fires started by the rioters, compounding the inmates' discomfort. This time, damage was estimated at around $100,000.

On December 29, fifteen of the ringleaders, their anger simmering, were transferred to cells in an underground segregation unit located beneath an unused barn. As reported by Global News in August 2018, veteran journalist and TV personality Jack Webster toured this area in 1988 and denounced it as a "disgusting, dingy, underground concrete dungeon," adding, "it doesn't belong in 1988. It belonged in 1888 or even 1788."

In the very early hours of New Year's Day 1988, allegedly thanks to a complicated manoeuvre involving a strip of sheeting and a sock weighted with peanuts, inmate Bruce McKay succeeded in unlatching his cell door. There were two junior guards on duty that night. After threatening one of them with a shank, McKay obtained the keys to the cells and set his fellows free.

A couple of the inmates refused to leave the bunker. Earl Andersen is convinced that one of them saved a guard's life. The guard "really thought he was going to die that night," Andersen told Global News in 2018. "And he may well have if the ... inmate hadn't basically intervened and said, 'Listen, you guys are free, away you go.'"

Thirteen maximum-security inmates, most of them charged with robbery, all of them dangerous, clambered over a fence and disappeared into the night.

The day after the escape, BCTV aired an interview with twenty-three-year-old Terry Hall, one of the escapees, who had undertaken to surrender at the end of the weekend. He blamed the guards for the riot. "You could smell the booze right on them," he said bitterly. "You can only push people so far, and I think this was pushing it right to the limit." A guard who was also interviewed at the time countered by accusing prisoners of spitting on prison staff, throwing things at them, and even urinating on food.

By January 4, nine of the thirteen prisoners were back in custody, with the remaining four apprehended in the weeks that followed. All were charged with escaping lawful custody.

To address issues arising from these incidents and calm the traumatized public, the provincial government launched a Royal Commission of Inquiry on January 6, with Judge Ian L. Drost at its head. The report concluded that the facility was overcrowded and dilapidated and the security was obsolete, and it advised the province to "close the doors of Oakalla forever."

Ironically, in spite of the fears of authorities and local residents, escapes petered out almost completely after that last explosive breakout. The solution to the problem was embarrassingly low-tech: stationing guard dogs and their handlers around the perimeter of the grounds.

However, the appalling events of December 1987 and January 1988 were to be the final straw. Also recorded in the 2018 Global News article was the opinion of former Burnaby mayor Derek Corrigan, who worked as a guard in Oakalla in the 1970s: "It was a place that generated economic activity, but then that corner turned and suddenly it became a deficit. People were worried about the prison and worried about the fact that it was right in the middle of what was a growing urban community."

At the end of June 1991, the last inmate was shipped out.

Before the wreckers moved in, however, the community threw a weekend-long party on the site, with proceeds of a "Jail House Rock" evening and a daytime carnival going toward the purchase of medical equipment for Burnaby Hospital.

Predictably, what replaced the much-reviled prison complex was a much-sought-after townhouse complex of more than five hundred units, overlooking Deer Lake and affording splendid views of the North Shore Mountains. Nowadays, homes for sale in Oakalla have a median listing price of more than $1,700,000.

And so, a mere eighty years after the people of Burnaby first voiced their objections to the construction of a prison farm on prime real estate in their neighbourhood, the community finally witnessed the end of an institution that, during its seventy-nine years of operation, had been the scene of devastating riots, escapes, deaths, and hangings.

Hauntingly, all that remains today is a granite staircase, once part of the main entrance, now leading nowhere.

POROUS WALLS

The granite staircase leading to the front door of the main block of Oakalla Prison. These stairs are the only part of the facility that remained after the prison was torn down in 1991 and replaced by a townhouse complex.

12

"Run, Bambi, Run"

The Troubling Case of Lawrencia Ann Bembenek

TO SAY THAT THE STAFF AND PATRONS OF THE COLUMBIA GRILL & Tavern in Thunder Bay, Ontario, were surprised when the news broke on Thursday, October 18, 1990, would be an understatement. They were gobsmacked. It was unthinkable that the young, attractive waitress who had been serving up scrambled eggs and coffee with a smile for the past three months was actually an escapee from a Wisconsin prison, and a convicted murderer at that!

"I can never believe in a million years that this girl did what they said she did," restaurant owner Louis Kebezes told *The Washington Post*. "She was an excellent employee. She was never late, and she worked anytime you asked her to work. I started her as a waitress, but after a month I let her go to the cash register, and left her alone."

The girl, who went by the name of Jennifer Lee Gazzana, was clearly American, "but she had a Canadian social insurance number, so what could I do?" said Kebezes.

Well, who was she?

Her real name was Lawrencia (she preferred Laurie) Ann Bembenek, and her fantastical life story reads like lurid pulp fiction.

It didn't start out that way. In fact, her early life was fairly uneventful. She was born in Milwaukee on August 15, 1958, the youngest daughter of Joe and Virginia Bembenek. Her father was a carpenter who had once worked as a police officer. Like so many kids, she found school boring, but she played the flute in the high school band and excelled on the track. She went to college. Thereafter, she worked briefly in retail, then as a model. A childhood friend remembers her as "always stunningly gorgeous."

In March 1980, Bembenek was accepted into the Milwaukee Police Academy. That was when things turned darker. In her 1992 memoir, *Woman on Trial*, she wrote of the abuse and harassment she had suffered during her training, complaining bitterly that Black or female recruits would be punished for minor offences, whereas white men escaped scot-free.

Within a month of starting to work for the Milwaukee Police Department (MPD), she was in deep trouble. A colleague and supposed friend, Judy Zess, was arrested at a concert for smoking marijuana, then fired. Zess claimed that Bembenek was equally guilty. Although Bembenek denied the accusation, she, too, lost her job.

Defiantly, but perhaps rashly, she decided to sue the MPD for sexual discrimination and began assisting authorities with an investigation into alleged corruption and fraud in the police department. She also caused a furor by handing the authorities a slew of colour photos of off-duty male police officers (bizarrely, one of them her future husband, Elfred "Fred" O. Schultz, whom she had not yet met) dancing nude in a public park.

After leaving the MPD, Bembenek found work at the Playboy Club in Lake Geneva, Wisconsin. Eventually, she took a job as a private security guard.

According to the *Milwaukee Journal Sentinel* in November 2010, she once said ruefully that "it's always a negative — if not a sexual — image they paint. I was a waitress at the Playboy Club for three weeks, but I'll always be known as the Playboy bunny." She had also, as was often emphasized in media reports, once posed in seductive attire for a Schlitz-beer calendar.

It was toward the middle of 1980 that she met Fred Schultz, a thirteen-year MPD veteran, recently divorced from his first wife, Christine. "I was drawn in by his overwhelming personality," wrote Bembenek.

The couple was married in January 1981. Even before the wedding, cracks had started to appear, connected both to Schultz's abusive behaviour and his obligations to pay his ex-wife alimony and child support.

Just four months later, in the early morning of May 28, Christine Schultz was murdered in her Milwaukee home. Gagged and blindfolded, her hands tied with rope, she was shot in the back at point-blank range with a single bullet from a .38-calibre pistol. Her two young sons witnessed the crime. The older boy, Sean, aged eleven, described the assailant as a hefty, masked man with a reddish-coloured ponytail, dressed in a green army jacket and black shoes. His younger brother, Shannon, aged seven, said that the intruder was wearing a green jogging suit.

Fred Schultz was called to the scene. He had been heard threatening his ex, but he had a seemingly rock-solid alibi that night — a colleague he'd been on duty with vouched for him — and, so, when ballistics testing suggested that the murder weapon was his off-duty revolver, suspicion fell on Bembenek. She had been alone that evening and had access to both the gun and a key to Christine's house. She was charged with murder in June 1981.

The case caused a sensation.

From the very beginning, Bembenek claimed that she had been framed as payback for filing the discrimination complaint and helping with investigations into allegations of corruption in the police force. At her trial, prosecutors asserted that she had killed Christine to rid the newly married couple of the financial burdens caused by Schultz's commitments to his ex-wife. The prosecution paraded a hodgepodge of facts, conjecture, and circumstantial evidence. Some significant examples: police had recovered a reddish-brown wig from a clogged drain in the accused's building, which may have come from either her apartment or the apartment next door, and a saleswoman testified that she'd sold

Bembenek a similar wig; several witnesses declared that they had seen Bembenek in a green outfit like the one described by Shannon Schultz, although Bembenek denied owning such a garment; and, most damning of all, Bembenek had access to the alleged murder weapon and, with no evidence of forced entry, the house key.

Under cross-examination, it is worth noting, Sean Schultz indicated that he believed the murderer was far too brawny to be Bembenek, even if she had been wearing football shoulder pads.

As reported in *Milwaukee Magazine* in 2011, the judge revealed after her trial: "This case was undoubtedly the most circumstantial case that I have seen." But for him, and the jury, the ballistics evidence was key. "Principally [with] the gun, the murder weapon in this case, [the evidence] wove an inescapable net of only one conclusion."

After four days, the jury returned their verdict: guilty of first-degree murder.

Bembenek's sentence was life imprisonment, to be served at the Taycheedah Correctional Institution, a maximum- and medium-security facility for adult female offenders in Fond du Lac, Wisconsin.

Fred Schultz initially stood by his wife. But soon after the trial he turned against her, saying that he now believed that she was "guilty as sin." His farewell letter, gleefully regurgitated in *People* magazine, read: "Dear Lawrencia: Goodbye. Good luck. Fred."

They were divorced in 1984. Schultz moved to Florida, where he remarried.

"I did love him, once," Bembenek commented in her memoir. "Then his jealousies and his lies enmeshed me."

As noted by Bob Drury and Marnie Inskip in a hard-hitting exclusive report, published in *Vanity Fair* in 1991, it was difficult to find anyone in Milwaukee, regardless of their stance on Bembenek's innocence or guilt, who had fond memories of Schultz. He was known to hang out with drug dealers and convicted felons. Then there was this: "One veteran cop recalls seeing Schultz standing with a group of friends before a line of cocaine that stretched the length of the twenty-foot bar in Tracks, the pub that sponsored the annual picnic at which the nude photos were taken."

Multiple appeals of Bembenek's murder conviction were denied. (According to *The Washington Post,* a lovestruck local man contributed the considerable sum of $28,000 toward the cost of her appeals.)

And so, on the evening of July 15, 1990, after serving eight years in Taycheedah with scant hope of parole, Bembenek, then thirty-two years old, broke free.

"When you're in one place for long enough, you start to know every inch of every room. You start to think, 'How can I get out of here?'" she told Jack Lakey in an exclusive for *The Toronto Star* in January 1991.

After the inmates were counted at 5.30 p.m., she took a load of her sweaty clothes to the prison laundry room in the basement. She then crawled through an opening in the window — around two-foot square, not six inches as asserted by prison officials, who, she claimed, "exaggerated the smallness of the window to minimize their fault" — before clambering over a seven-foot-high fence topped with barbed wire and disappearing into the dusk.

Waiting on the other side of the wire with an idling automobile, as prearranged, was thirty-four-year-old Dominic Gugliatto, a divorced factory worker with three children. The couple had met when Gugliatto visited a relative in prison, and they had become engaged.

"It did feel a bit like Bonnie and Clyde," Bembenek told Drury and Inskip with a smile.

Her dramatic breakout catapulted her to folk-hero status in her home state. A crowd of three hundred joined a rally to celebrate her escape. According to a phone-in survey conducted by a local TV station, five out of every six Milwaukeeans thought she had been wrongly convicted. She was popularly known as Bambi by then (although she hated the name), and her legion of supporters produced bumper stickers and a range of T-shirts, all adorned with the slogan "Run, Bambi, Run."

In her interview with Jack Lakey in 1991, Bembenek spoke wistfully of the brief window of freedom she enjoyed in Thunder Bay, then a city of around 114,000 residents. "Looking back, they were the three best months of my life. It was living on the edge, but it was worth it to me. I was at the point where I had absolutely nothing to lose."

Armed with forged IDs, Bembenek and Gugliatto introduced themselves to folks in Thunder Bay as Jennifer and Tony Gazzana from Chicago, looking for an escape from "big-city violence." She took a job at the Columbia Grill, and a second at a fitness centre. Gugliatto worked sporadically.

Bembenek enthused about the "visually stimulating" world she encountered on the north shore of Lake Superior, but "one of my favourite things was to just go for a walk at night. At the prison we were only allowed to go out into the little exercise yard during the day, so I really missed just being outside at night."

But the window slammed shut when her story was featured in an episode of Fox's TV show *America's Most Wanted*. Subsequently, the network received a call from "a California viewer vacationing in Thunder Bay." Shocked, perhaps, at spotting a familiar face at a local restaurant but clearly anxious to do his civic duty, the man informed authorities in both Canada and the United States.

On October 17, 1990, a Thunder Bay police officer turned up at Bembenek's workplace to ask her a few questions. Later that day, the RCMP followed up with an official visit to her basement apartment, where she and Gugliatto were packing in a panic, frantic to get out of town. "It was very sad, but they were quite nice, very civil about it," Bembenek told Lakey. "Nobody threw us down on the floor to handcuff us, like at home. One cop was worried about what would happen to our cat."

As per *The Washington Post*, her ex-husband commented after her recapture that he felt "like the Packers won the Super Bowl. It's awesome."

Dominic Gugliatto was deported to Wisconsin, facing charges of aiding and abetting an escape from lawful custody. Their relationship, severely tested while they were on the run, soon sputtered and died.

So Bembenek found herself behind bars again, initially at the Thunder Bay District Jail, then at the Metropolitan Toronto West Detention Centre. In her memoir, she described Metro West as "a very punitive environment." It was "just a holding tank, a detention center, never meant for long stays.... It has no humanity. You can't go anywhere, you can't do anything, you can't have anything — any of the little creature comforts that you might have had in other prisons are forbidden."

A Canadian attorney, Frank Marrocco, took up the cudgels for her. He argued that she should be granted asylum in Canada as a political prisoner, and that she was being persecuted by a conspiracy between the police department and the judicial system in Wisconsin.

Lawyers were not the only Canadians who came to Bembenek's defence.

In September 1991, Louis Kebezes, who had so vigorously spoken out for his employee after her arrest, put up her bail of $10,000. She was at large for exactly one night before Wisconsin began extradition proceedings, and she was rearrested. Bembenek was outraged when, despite multiple requests submitted to Canadian immigration officials by the restaurateur and a clutch of helpful lawyers, Kebezes was still waiting for his refund nearly ten months later. As a result, one of his restaurants had gone insolvent.

At that point, an exceptionally eminent Canadian stepped into the fray. Peter John Vickers Worthington, founder and former editor-in-chief of *The Toronto Sun*, wrote a searing piece for the *Sun* entitled "The squeezing of Louis Kebezes." Were the authorities "showing contempt for a citizen's rights" in an attempt to discourage others from putting up bail in immigration cases? Nine days later, perhaps by sheer coincidence, the *Sun* was able to run a story with the headline "Bambi pal finally paid back."

"Was Bambi Framed?" asked Drury and Inskip in their 1991 *Vanity Fair* article. There were so many tangled threads to the sensational story of "Lawrencia Bembenek, former model, ex-Milwaukee police officer, and either the remorseless killer of her husband's first wife, the most winsome charlatan to sway men's souls since Mme. Blavatsky [Russian/American sage or fraud, depending on who you ask], or Political Prisoner No. 889275104, the victim of a byzantine plot whose elements are a murky farrago of pinup calendars, homicide, cocaine, police corruption, loopy paramours, and a dramatic jailbreak."

The Canadian government agreed to Bembenek's extradition, subject to a commitment by Wisconsin authorities to review her case. In April 1992, she voluntarily returned to Taycheedah.

As a consequence of the review, she was awarded a new trial. She decided to strike a deal with prosecutors, pleading no contest to second-degree murder. This was tantamount to a get-out-of-jail card, although it was not free. Her sentence was twenty years; she was released on parole for time served. Later, she explained that this seemed to be her only option if she wanted to spend time with her parents, who were in failing health. But, in retrospect, it seems to have been another in a long series of unfortunate life choices.

Again, her celebrity spiked. She became the subject of movies. She appeared on TV and talk shows, including Oprah Winfrey's. She wrote an autobiography, painted and sold her paintings, and gave speeches.

Laurie Bembenek, a talented artist, posing with one of the works she painted while in prison. The photograph was taken in the early 1990s by Peter Worthington of *The Toronto Sun*.

But she could never escape her troubled past. Or her ill luck.

She was arrested for possession of marijuana. She filed for bankruptcy. A gallery where her artwork was on display burned down; everything was destroyed. Bizarrely, while being sequestered with a bodyguard in an apartment ahead of an appearance on the *Dr. Phil* show in 2002, she had a panic attack and tried to climb out of a window. She fell, injuring her right foot so severely that it had to be amputated. A second marriage ended in divorce.

On November 21, 2010, Laurie Bembenek died in hospice care in Portland, Oregon, after suffering liver and kidney failure, complicated by post-traumatic stress disorder and alcoholism. She was just fifty-two years old.

Ex-cop turned private investigator Ira Robins spent decades trying to prove Bembenek's innocence. He persevered, even after she died. According to *The Chronicle-Journal* in 2016, he said, "I want it to be that nothing like this ever happens to anyone in the state of Wisconsin again."

There is no question that Christine Schultz was most foully murdered. What has come under increasing scrutiny over the years is: Who did it?

Fred Schultz had an alibi for the night of the murder, although it was later shown to be not nearly as airtight as first believed. He could have been involved directly — or indirectly, perhaps by hiring someone to execute his ex-wife. His motive could have been to rid himself of that financial albatross around his neck, or to pay Bembenek back for submitting to his superiors those embarrassing photos of him cavorting in the nude — or both. Could the killer have been Frederick Horenberger, who was known to Schultz and his circle, and who was arrested for carrying out an armed robbery during which he had worn a ponytailed wig and gagged the victim? After his death by suicide in 1991, several people alleged that Horenberger had confessed to the killing. And what about Judy Zess, Bembenek's so-called friend who had ratted her out to the MPD? Zess had previously lived in Schultz and Bembenek's apartment. She may have kept a key and thus had access to the alleged murder weapon. And speaking of the murder weapon — the vital piece of evidence that sank Bembenek at her trial in 1981 — four forensic experts brought in by Canadian lawyer Marrocco in the early 1990s concluded that it could not have been the gun that fired the fatal shot.

On all these questions, the jury of judicial — and public — opinion is still out.

What is certain is that beautiful and doomed Laurie Bembenek has been moved out of the frame. Sadly, despite a years-long battle, she never succeeded in having her sentence overturned.

Bembenek may have described her time in Thunder Bay as "the three best months" of her life, but things are never that simple. "I can't tell you how hard it is living on the run," she lamented in her book, adding, "I was scared all the time, in fact." She came to realize that "if I am to win my freedom, it will have to be here [in Milwaukee], where they first took it from me."

The book, published in 1992, ends with these words:

> Going on is possible.
> Survival is possible.
> Even happiness is possible, I hope.
> But I'm not at all sure about forgiveness.

13

Blade Runners

Audacious Escapes by Helicopter

IN MARCH 2016, THE INTERNET LIT UP WITH A VIDEO OF TWO MEN dangling perilously at the end of a rope. The six-minute-long footage had been shot three years previously but was initially kept under wraps.

On the afternoon of Sunday, March 17, 2013, Sébastien Foray, a twenty-nine-year-old freshly licensed helicopter pilot stationed at Mont-Tremblant, Quebec, was hired at the going rate of $800 to take two men on a tour of the majestic Laurentian region to the north of Montreal. Once the four-seater Robinson R44 was airborne, the "tourists" dropped all pretense of interest in the spectacular snow-covered scenery. Instead, they brandished a pistol and ordered Foray to head for nearby Saint-Jérôme detention centre, a provincial facility that housed 480 inmates and was regarded as being critically overcrowded and dismally understaffed on weekends.

When Foray tried to alert air traffic control, the hijackers ripped off his headset.

A witness called what followed a real "James Bond moment," although James Bond would probably have cringed at the comparison. The helicopter pilot could certainly not be faulted: though under extreme duress, he landed his craft with pinpoint precision on the roof of the prison. Thereupon, his unwelcome passengers threw a rope over the wall to a couple of inmates waiting in the yard below. Despite, or perhaps because of, the clumsy and increasingly desperate attempts of their accomplices on the rooftop, the escapees weren't able to clamber aboard the chopper. After several nail-biting minutes, as shown in the video filmed by Saint-Jérôme surveillance cameras, the helicopter took off and faded from view with two figures swaying on the rope beneath.

Astonishingly, the guards on duty at the time did nothing to interfere with the escape. The union president of Peace Officers in Correctional Services of Quebec was quoted by CBC News in March 2016 as saying, "We have to evaluate who's on board the helicopter — they were accomplices. Were they armed? We cannot intervene with inmates climbing a rope. It's only in the movies that you can shoot down a helicopter with a handgun."

The dangling duo were identified as thirty-six-year-old Benjamin Hudon-Barbeau and Dany Provençal, thirty-three. According to *The Globe and Mail*, Hudon-Barbeau depicted himself as an innocent living in mortal fear of what might happen to him while behind bars — hence his burning desire to escape. Well, he was perhaps not entirely innocent. In addition to a previous acquittal of a murder conviction on appeal, he was believed to have ties to the Hells Angels.

From small beginnings in Quebec in the 1970s, the Hells Angels Motorcycle Club, described by Criminal Intelligence Service Canada (CISC) as "an international outlaw motorcycle gang," has extended its reach throughout the country. According to CISC, outlaw motorcycle gangs have their fingers in multiple felonious pies such as fraud, theft, drug trafficking, prostitution, illegal gambling, extortion, intimidation, and murder. In 2004, the Hells Angels was singled out as the most powerful of these gangs with thirty-four chapters across Canada. A 2016 article in *Vice* magazine noted that the Hells Angels was by far the biggest biker club in the country, bigger than all the other criminal clubs combined.

A four-seater Robinson R44, similar to the helicopter hijacked in March 2013 to free Benjamin Hudon-Barbeau and Dany Provençal from the Saint-Jérôme detention centre in Quebec.

As stated by the police, Hudon-Barbeau had again been arrested in 2012 and was awaiting trial on firearms-related charges in connection with a double homicide in the Laurentians. His fellow-escapee, Dany Provençal, was serving a nine-year sentence for arson and home invasion. Reportedly, Hudon-Barbeau and his confrères on the outside had used mobile devices to coordinate the escape.

Next stop for the whirlybird was a rough field a short distance away from the prison. Once again displaying extraordinary skill, Foray landed after lowering the two men gently to the ground — one of them, according to *The Globe and Mail*, hanging upside-down — thus enabling them to climb aboard the helicopter. The final destination was a hotel parking lot in Estérel, where a white Cadillac SUV was waiting to whisk the fugitives away. The rattled pilot managed to fly back to base, and he was treated for shock at the local hospital.

An armed contingent of police officers was soon in hot pursuit of the escapees.

The chase ended in the small resort village of Chertsey, some fifty kilometres north of Saint-Jérôme, where, after a fierce exchange of gunfire with police, the suspects forced their way into a lakeside cabin. The panicked homeowners fled out the back door.

"This is a sportsman's paradise, a nice place to cross-country ski or go fishing," lamented a local resident in the March 19, 2013, edition of *The Montreal Gazette*. "I can't imagine what our poor neighbours had to go through, hiding behind a snowbank, not knowing if it's safe to come out."

By 8:30 p.m., Hudon-Barbeau and the two hijackers had been arrested. The following morning, Provençal surrendered without incident.

In 2015, Provençal entered a guilty plea to the charge of escaping from prison, and another seven years were tacked onto his existing sentence. A year later, Hudon-Barbeau was sentenced to sixteen years after pleading guilty to charges of theft of an aircraft, escape from prison, breaking and entering, and theft and damage of property.

But for Hudon-Barbeau, there was worse to come.

In 2017, he was convicted of first-degree murder, second-degree murder, and two counts of attempted murder for the 2012 homicides in the Laurentians, ending up with a life sentence and no chance of parole for thirty-five years. This was the longest sentence ever imposed in Quebec. To his great good fortune, though, the Quebec Court of Appeal revisited his case in 2023, after the Supreme Court of Canada had ruled that imposing consecutive sentences for multiple murders was unconstitutional. He could now be eligible for parole after twenty-five rather than thirty-five years.

////////////////

In 2014, just fifteen months after the Saint-Jérôme spectacle, an event came about that authorities in Quebec should have anticipated and prevented — a copycat escape by helicopter, this time from the province-run medium-security Quebec Detention Centre in Quebec City, also known as the Prison d'Orsainville, which was home to some seven hundred inmates.

It's worth noting that this was not the first time that chopper blades had whirred in the environs of Orsainville, with a hijacker attempting to coerce a pilot into springing a convict from captivity.

On May 7, 1981, a young woman hired a helicopter in Sainte-Foy, Quebec City, claiming that she wanted to take aerial photographs of nearby Orsainville Zoo. Once in the air, the woman's true motive was revealed. As the pilot, Brian Jenner, said later, she grabbed his headset, pointed a sawed-off .12-gauge shotgun at his head, and ordered him to land at Orsainville prison.

Media outlets worldwide pounced on the story. For example, *The Honolulu Advertiser* quoted Jenner two days after the incident: "She said she wanted to free her husband from jail. But I told her I wouldn't land there because there were armed guards at the jail, and there could be shooting."

Jenner also calmly told the woman, later identified as twenty-five-year-old Marina Paquet of Quebec City, that if she shot him the helicopter would crash and they would both die. Police afterward confirmed that her husband was in jail pending extradition to the United States in connection with a robbery and murder in California.

Paquet, who Jenner described as "fairly cool," finally turned her gun over to him and agreed to return to Sainte-Foy. Once the helicopter touched down, she tried to make a run for it. In vain: within minutes, she was arrested and subsequently charged with extortion, forcible detention, and the illegal use of a firearm.

The breakout at Orsainville on June 7, 2014, however, was markedly more successful. As was widely reported, it all took less than a minute. At approximately 7:43 p.m., a helicopter dropped out of the sky into one of the prison yards. Three men hopped aboard, and the chopper (according to some sources a nimble Robinson R44, similar to the one used in the previous year's break from Saint-Jérôme) took off, heading in a westerly direction.

At a stroke, three "extremely dangerous" inmates were on the loose.

The fugitives were Yves Denis, aged thirty-five, Denis Lefebvre, fifty-three, and forty-nine-year-old Serge Pomerleau. Pomerleau was regarded as the kingpin of a massive organized-crime ring that had been based in Val-d'Or, in the Abitibi-Témiscamingue region of northwestern Quebec, with suspected links to the Quebec Hells Angels. The trio had been arrested in 2010 during a drug bust dubbed Opération Écrevisse (Project Crawfish). They were currently facing a slew of charges, including gangsterism and trafficking in cocaine, marijuana, and amphetamines. They were also slated to stand trial in 2015 for the slaying of several rivals in a turf war.

News of the escape triggered an extensive manhunt, with Interpol issuing a global alert.

As it turned out, the services of Interpol were not required. The reason, as a CNN reporter observed dryly, was that they evidently did not fly far enough. Just as far as Montreal, where they were found two weeks after their escape hunkering down in a luxury tenth-floor condo in Old Montreal.

The SWAT team involved in their early Sunday morning capture was clearly not in the mood for politeness. Canadian Press images taken in the aftermath show that the door had been bashed in and the interior turned upside-down.

It became apparent that the fugitives had not been deprived of the finer things in life. There were flowers in a vase, and police reported finding new clothing and delicacies such as shrimp and other seafood, as well as $100,000 in cash, probably to help the escapees get out of Canada. They were not armed and did not resist arrest.

By Sunday evening, the trio was safely tucked back in Orsainville. In October 2014, they were all found guilty of a slew of drug and gangsterism offences.

In the immediate wake of the breakout, prison authorities, police, and politicians scrambled to deal with the fallout.

The president of the union representing Quebec prison guards took issue with criticism that guards had failed to spring into action once the helicopter was spotted: "The rules of engagement do not allow us to fire on a vehicle, let alone a helicopter," *The Globe and Mail* reported him as saying two days after the breakout. He also lashed out at the Ministry of Public Security for failing to take preventative measures after the 2013 incident; in particular, for not installing metal cables over prison yards to prevent helicopters from landing, a system followed in the United States and several European countries.

What made it even more galling for the authorities was that court documents subsequently revealed that months before the break the Sûreté du Québec (SQ) had alerted prison officials to the fact that the three men represented a flight risk. On their arrival at Orsainville in March 2014, they had initially been given the highest security rating, but within weeks their security had been relaxed to the extent that Pomerleau had a laptop in his cell, ostensibly to help him prepare for his trial, and all three of them — together, and free of handcuffs and leg shackles — were given access to a less-secure exercise courtyard.

"It is incomprehensible," fumed police analyst Stéphane Berthomet in the *Globe* on June 24. "Why was their security rating decreased? How could hardened criminals become lambs within a few months? These were dangerous people who wanted to escape. It defies common sense."

The prison warden blamed a Quebec Superior Court judge for the reclassification. The judge had been concerned that protests by defence lawyers against the accused men's strict detention conditions might derail the trial.

Provincial politicians, too, were squabbling. The opposition Parti Québécois (PQ), as reported in *The Montreal Gazette* on June 12, described the handling of the incident by Public Security Minister Lise Thériault as a "lamentable failure." In turn, Thériault accused the PQ, which had been in power at the time of the previous helicopter incident in 2013, of not taking any corrective action back then. Liberal Premier Philippe Couillard stepped in to defend his minister, calling for an independent inquiry into both escapes. With four administrative levels involved: public security, the prison administration, the SQ, and the justice ministry, "the government is not satisfied with the flow of information, of the coordination of information, of certain contradictory elements in this," he said.

///////////////

The events of June 7, 2014, brought back searing memories for Fred Fandrich of Hope, British Columbia. "Quite frankly this (news) scared the s--- right out of me," he told Douglas Quan, in a *Montreal Gazette* story published on June 12, 2014.

Fandrich's ordeal had started when he arrived at his Hope-based business, Valley Helicopters, at 7:30 a.m. on June 18, 1990. There, he was accosted by a masked gunman, who forced him to take to the skies in his Bell 206 helicopter. About thirty minutes into the flight, Fandrich was given his destination: Kent Institution, an all-male federal maximum-security prison located in Agassiz, BC, about 130 kilometres east of Vancouver and thirty-three west of Hope. According to an Associated Press report at the time, Kent housed some of the most dangerous criminals in Canada, with around half of the inmates in protective custody and a quarter serving life sentences.

One of those lifers was Robert Lee Ford, a thirty-two-year-old Vancouver Island drug-lord-turned-murderer. As Fandrich hovered the helicopter over a yard just inside the perimeter fence, the hijacker opened fire on a corrections officer in a truck, hitting him in the knee. Ford ran through a gate and scaled an interior fence before clambering aboard the chopper. He was accompanied by David Thomas, twenty-four, serving an eight-year term for robbery.

Lori Stevens, who lived across the road from the prison, watched the action unfold from the comfort of her living room. "It was fun to watch. It looked like a bad movie," she told AP News after the incident.

The traumatized pilot didn't see things in quite the same way. "There was a lot of gunfire inside the helicopter from the guy with the gun and it was very, very loud when he's shooting a foot away from your head," he said.

Justifiably anxious about what would happen next, Fandrich followed instructions to the letter, landing the helicopter at Silver Creek, just west of Hope. To his relief, the escapees merely sat him down on one of the copter's skids and tied him up. After freeing himself, Fandrich contacted the police.

Two days later, the RCMP found Ford and Thomas hiding on a heavily wooded island on nearby Harrison Lake. The police opened fire. Bullets punched holes into Thomas's sweatshirt. Both men were lucky to escape injury. After their arrest, they were placed in administrative segregation, better known as solitary confinement, and subsequently charged with prison break. The hijacker, Allan Jupp, was convicted for helping them to get away.

///////////////////

An entertaining online analysis by blogger Tosin George reveals that Canada's tally of four whirlybird escapes between 1971 and 2020 — three successful

(Kent Institution 1990, Saint-Jérôme 2013, and Orsainville 2014) and one unsuccessful (Orsainville 1981) — compares favourably with that of Greece and Belgium, but lags behind the United States, which has a total of eight.

When it comes to audacious aerial getaways, though, no one can top the French. They registered an astonishing fifteen prison break attempts by helicopter within that time period, eleven of them successful.

Several examples stand out above the rest.

You will remember "Le grand gangster" Jacques Mesrine's escape in 1978 from La Santé, Paris's fortress prison. In 1986, an even more dramatic escape would embarrass the authorities at that penal institution, purported to be one of the most secure in the world. At around 10:30 a.m. on May 26, an Alouette II helicopter came to a stop, hovering just above the pitched roof of one of the prison buildings. At the controls was Nadine Vaujour, who had trained as a pilot for the sole purpose of liberating her husband, Michel, who was then serving eighteen years for armed robbery and attempted murder. Within moments, two men emerged and clambered up the roof toward the copter. No shots were fired, reportedly because the guards' sightlines were obstructed by a large chimney. Vaujour climbed onto the craft alone; his partner was either left behind or had second thoughts about leaving. A few minutes later, the helicopter landed and was abandoned in a sports field in the south of Paris, where a car was waiting to whisk the couple away.

Vaujour was recaptured five months later. In a shootout with police during a bank robbery, he took a bullet to the head that left him partly paralyzed, although he did eventually claw his way back to health.

When it came to escapes by helicopter, however, Michel Vaujour couldn't hold a candle to his countryman Pascal Payet. Convicted murderer Payet (dubbed "the frequent flyer" by CNN) holds the record for orchestrating the highest number of chopper escapes — five! He seems to have been equally at home breaking out himself and helping others to break out.

The series began in 2001, when, with the assistance of an accomplice, he fled via helicopter from Luynes penitentiary in southern France. In 2003, while still on the run, he used a chopper to help three others escape from the same prison. His most impressive getaway took place in 2007, when he was once again behind bars — this time in solitary confinement at the state penitentiary in Grasse. Four masked and heavily armed associates hijacked a helicopter from Cannes airport and forced the pilot to land on the roof of the prison. After busting Payet out, the group fled to Brignoles in southeastern France, where the pilot was released unharmed. Payet did not have very long to relish his freedom. Two months later, he was recaptured in Spain.

If there were a French Escape-by-Helicopter Hall of Fame, the third inductee would have to be armed robber, jewel thief, and convicted murderer Rédoine Faïd, once nominated as France's public enemy number one. Although he escaped just twice and only once by helicopter, both instances were sensational. In April 2013, he broke out of jail in Lille by producing a pistol from a bag, taking four prison guards hostage, and using explosives to blast his way through four gates to reach a waiting vehicle in the prison car park.

In July 2018, Faïd was serving time in Réau prison, fifty kilometres southeast of Paris. In vintage Hollywood style, two armed and masked men hijacked an Alouette II helicopter from an airfield east of Paris and forced the terrified pilot to fly to Réau. When the pilot encountered problems with the rickety machine, the hijackers beat him and threatened to harm his family. ("I wasn't resisting; I didn't have any choice with two Colts held to my head," the pilot told *The Guardian*'s Kim Willsher soon after the event.) While the chopper hovered just above a small triangular courtyard in the prison, the only one that was net-free, the attackers dropped to the ground, set off smoke bombs to confuse prison guards, and cut through a door using an angle grinder. They located Faïd in the visitor's room and spirited him away.

The helicopter was later found, partially burned out, near Gonesse to the northeast of Paris. The pilot was treated in hospital for shock. Faïd was at liberty for three months before being arrested in Creil, his birthplace in northern France.

As a career criminal, serial jailbreaker, self-promoter, author, and master of disguise — while on the run in the 1990s, he masqueraded as an Orthodox Jew in Israel, and, after his 2018 escape, wore a burka to move around in public — Faïd has been admiringly compared to Jacques Mesrine.

In 2023, the so-called getaway king received a fourteen-year sentence for the 2018 breakout. As reported in *The Guardian* in October of that year,

Faïd told the court that his desire to escape was triggered by the thought of spending some twenty more years in jail, which was like a "concrete coffin" and "boring as hell." With this time added to his existing sentences, though, he could conceivably remain inside until 2060.

///////////////

It is clear that helicopters have their limitations. You have to own, borrow, rent, or hijack a (possibly undependable) machine, then fly it into a hostile environment, with no guarantee that the vulnerable contraption won't crash or be shot out of the skies, with fatal consequences for all on board.

So what's next on the horizon for aerial prison breakouts? Could unmanned aerial vehicles or drones be a possibility?

Certainly drones, programmed via cellphones, are already widely in use to drop wire cutters and other handy tools into prisons and otherwise facilitate escapes — for example, French authorities believed that Rédoine Faïd's associates had flown drones over Réau prison in 2018 to familiarize themselves with the layout prior to carrying out the raid.

Sizable drones capable of carrying humans are already in development — in 2023, according to U.S. business magazine *Forbes*, an autonomous passenger drone received safety and airworthiness approval in China. But even when this technology is fully developed and globally deployed, it would be a real stretch to believe that drones would be more successful than helicopters in effecting escapes by landing in prisons or hovering over roofs or jail yards and unspooling ropes to hoist inmates to freedom.

The bottom line is that there were reportedly forty-eight helicopter-assisted prison escapes and escape attempts worldwide between 1971 and 2020. That is a minuscule number when compared to the many other tried and tested methods, such as sawing through window bars, cutting through fences, climbing over walls, or, simplest and most effective of all, just walking away.

14

Island Retreat

Bordeaux Prison: The First Hundred Years

OVER THE YEARS, THE MONTREAL DETENTION CENTRE, FORMERLY (and still informally) known as Bordeaux Prison, has had its fair share of escapes.

Bordeaux Prison is a provincial facility housing male inmates sentenced to two years or less or awaiting trial or transfer to another institution. It was built in the early 1900s in Bordeaux (now the borough of Ahuntsic-Cartierville) on the Island of Montreal as a replacement for the city's obsolete and dangerously overcrowded Pied-du-Courant prison, which dated back to the 1830s.

The moving force behind the establishment of the new prison was the last governor of the old one, Charles-Amédée Vallée, who tapped into the progressive penal theories of his time, including the belief that prisons were places for reforming offenders and that solitary confinement coupled with hard work were essential elements to effect reform. In their book *Bordeaux: L'histoire d'une prison*, Sébastien Bossé and Chantal Bouchard note that Vallée found the perfect expression of his vision in the Eastern State Penitentiary in Pennsylvania.

Shades of Toronto's historic Don Jail, constructed some fifty years prior: Bordeaux took years longer to build than anticipated — it eventually opened in 1912 — and soaring costs made a mockery of the budget. After an initial estimate of $750,000, the eventual price tag hovered around the $2.5 million mark — equivalent in purchasing power to around $65,500,000 today.

Following the Eastern State or Pennsylvania model, the prison was constructed in a "hub-and-spoke" formation, with six wings fanning out from a central twelve-sided domed tower. Windowed cells for convicted inmates, measuring 2 by 3.4 metres, were arranged along both sides of four of the six wings, with passageways down the centre. The fifth wing contained slightly larger cells to accommodate prisoners awaiting trial, and the sixth wing included visitors' rooms and the hospital section.

Vallée regarded the central tower as the beating heart of the institution. Conforming to the Eastern State requirement of constant surveillance, nothing could escape the attention of the guard always stationed there, making it "the best surveillance system imaginable."

There were also state-of-the-art workshops, and other structures within the compound included a guardhouse and an administration building. The whole complex was enclosed by two separate boundary walls.

By the time the prison "welcomed" its first one hundred inmates in 1912, the project had already weathered several scandals. One in particular, whipped up by the press, drove the locals crazy.

You might think the reason for their fury was having this huge, octopus-shaped structure designed to house hundreds of inmates of all levels of criminality literally in their back yard. But no. What incensed them was that jailbirds confined in their tiny cells would be enjoying up-to-the-minute comforts — a metal bed, a small desk, a flushing toilet, electric lighting, even! Far better facilities than those generally available to law-abiding citizens on the outside.

ISLAND RETREAT

An aerial view of Bordeaux Prison in 1929, showing the "hub-and-spoke" layout, with six wings fanning out from a central twelve-sided domed tower, and the two boundary walls.

Between 1914 and 1960, Bordeaux became the go-to place for capital punishment in Quebec. As at the Don Jail in Toronto, there was a death row consisting of four cells to accommodate murderers awaiting execution. Eighty-two hangings took place there, each signalled by the solemn tolling of the prison bell.

Three cases in particular marked significant stepping stones on the rough path to the abolition of capital punishment in Canada. In 1935, Canada's most famous (or infamous) hangman, Arthur Ellis, was tasked with the execution of Tommasina Teolis, who had hired two hitmen to kill her husband. Due to a fatal miscalculation of the length of rope required for the procedure, Teolis was beheaded. This provoked outrage on a global scale and led to two significant changes: the public was banned from viewing executions, and Ellis was shunned. His steady stream of jobs dried up, and he died in poverty three years later. In 1953, Marguerite Ruest Pitre was hanged at Bordeaux for her part in the downing of a commercial airplane and the deaths of the twenty-three passengers and crew. She would be the last woman to hang in Canada. And in 1956, amid huge controversy, Gaspé prospector and woodsman Wilbert Coffin was executed for the murder of an American bear hunter. Many believed at the time, and still do, that Coffin was wrongfully convicted and that the real killer or killers had walked free.

The first reliably documented escape from Bordeaux dates back to 1916. Clearly unimpressed with the metal bed and other features of his supposedly palatial quarters, a certain Joseph Masse fled from the prison farm, which was situated outside the prison enclosure. He was recaptured three days later.

By the time Bordeaux celebrated its hundredth anniversary, it was estimated that some ninety individuals had succeeded in escaping. The year 1938, for example, saw the departure from the hospital of an armed and dangerous fivesome, who took advantage of a ladder conveniently left behind by painters. One of the escapees was wounded and immediately taken back into custody. His fellows were apprehended a few days later, to the great relief of the fearful citizens of Montreal.

The 1960s were particularly challenging for the staff at Bordeaux — between July 1960 and September 1962, fifteen inmates flew the coop, most of them from the hospital area. But the two most newsworthy escapes of the period took place in 1965 and 1969.

///////////////////////

On March 2, 1965, André Durocher, serving a sentence of five years for robbery, requested permission to water the jail's ice-skating rink. The staff member in charge, Sergeant Roger Beaupré, asked a guard to accompany Durocher and fellow inmate Lucien Rivard to the boiler room to bring out some hoses. According to *The Montreal Gazette*, Quebec Attorney General Claude Wagner stated in his official report to the Legislative Assembly the following day, "Sgt. Beaupré did not give any thought at all to the fact it was very mild outside and that it would be futile to water the rink."

Once in the boiler room, Durocher produced a fake gun — described by Wagner as "a wooden imitation covered with shoe polish." The two prisoners disarmed the guard and bound him hand and foot. Two furnacemen suffered the same fate. It would take about an hour for the three men to free themselves and sound the alarm. By that time, Durocher and Rivard had subdued an armed guard on the inner west wall of the prison. After tying him up, the pair used a ladder to climb from the interior wall to the larger exterior wall, with the hoses serving as ropes for their descent on the other side. There, they hijacked a car and forced the driver, Jacques Bourgeois, to speed away. After taking his telephone number, they gave Bourgeois money for cab fare and dropped him off. Some thirty minutes later, Bourgeois received a courtesy call from the hijackers, informing him of the location of his abandoned vehicle.

At the time of the escape, twenty-eight-year-old André Durocher was serving his five-year term at Saint-Vincent-de-Paul Penitentiary in Laval but had been transferred to Bordeaux to await a hearing on another robbery charge. However, the spotlight of parliamentary, media, and public attention was not trained upon this man, whom a Sûreté du Québec (SQ) officer dismissed as "a small-time hood," but on his jailbreak partner, forty-nine-year-old Lucien Rivard, a career criminal with ties to the Montreal underworld.

At the time, Rivard was fighting extradition to the United States to face heroin smuggling charges. His case had already had a ripple effect in the political sphere, with an aide to the Canadian federal immigration minister being accused of attempting to secure Rivard's release on bail by offering a $20,000 bribe to a lawyer acting for the U.S. Additional senior ministerial staff members also allegedly used their influence in efforts to get bail for Rivard, as did Rivard's wife and others in his circle.

The scandal shook Prime Minister Lester B. Pearson's Liberal government, sparking the appointment of Quebec Chief Justice Frédéric Dorion as commissioner of a special public inquiry into bribery and influence-peddling at the highest levels of power. In addition to apportioning blame to various government officials and to the RCMP for an inadequate investigation, the Dorion report, tabled in the House of Commons on June 29, 1965, noted that Rivard's wife and associates had conspired to obstruct the course of justice.

In particular, the report criticized Federal Justice Minister Guy Favreau's handling of what became known as the "Rivard affair." The minister should have obtained the advice of his legal department before deciding not to prosecute in the case.

On the day the report was published, Favreau resigned as justice minister. Although he was subsequently appointed president of the Privy Council, a government advisory body, his political reputation was in tatters. He died in 1967, a broken man.

The late judge Jules Deschênes was Favreau's lawyer during the affair. As noted in a *Globe and Mail* article in February 2002, Deschênes once said, "I'm certain the scandal killed him."

Lucien Rivard's criminal record dated back to 1933, when, as a seventeen-year-old, he was arrested for breaking into a storage shed. He had come a long way since then, with links to the Mafia and Corsican smugglers. After a sojourn in Cuba running a casino (and guns for Fidel Castro's rebels), he returned to Quebec. He bought a half-interest in a resort in Laval, which was alleged to be a front for his multi-million-dollar smuggling business.

In October 1963, after having Rivard in their sights for years, police finally succeeded in linking him to a major crime. U.S. agents in Laredo, Texas, caught a drug runner attempting to bring thirty-five kilograms of heroin into the country from Mexico. The man fingered Rivard as one of the ringleaders of the operation, and Rivard was arrested in Montreal.

In the wake of Rivard's brazen prison break in March 1965, Quebec Premier Jean Lesage commented darkly that something strange had been going on. It turned out that the racketeer had not exactly been roughing it during his stay at Bordeaux. Reportedly, he did not sleep in a cell but in a comfortable room equipped with a television, where he enjoyed food and drink supplied by high-end restaurants. With the stench of corruption in the air, seven prison staff members, including the assistant governor, were suspended pending a probe into their roles in the affair.

The escape of the narcotics kingpin triggered the largest manhunt in Montreal police history. Despite the offer of a substantial reward, however, Rivard's trail seemed to go cold. Interpol reported that he might be in Peru, and, among others, his wife received letters that had been mailed in Spain and Mexico and Vancouver.

Three months after the breakout, Durocher was apprehended without incident in a north-end apartment in Montreal.

Finally, success: in mid-July, Rivard, now sporting long black hair and a full beard, was nabbed by police at a cottage on Lake Saint-Louis, some thirty kilometres to the southwest of Montreal. Just like his fellow jailbreaker, Rivard had never left the province.

Rivard was swiftly extradited to the U.S., where he was found guilty on two counts of conspiring to smuggle drugs. His sentence was twenty years plus a fine of $20,000.

After serving just less than ten years, Rivard returned to Canada and dropped out of the spotlight. In 2002, he died in Laval aged eighty-six, remembered as the man who, in the 1960s, nearly brought down the Liberal government.

////////////////////

In October 1969, the escape from custody of twenty-three-year-old Richard Blass, together with eight companions, caused a furor both at home and abroad. Montreal-born Blass was nicknamed "Le Chat" (The Cat) for his remarkable ability to hang on to life through multiple assassination attempts by the Italian Mafia, escapes from custody, and a police shootout.

Facing a long stretch in prison for wounding a police officer during a bank robbery in January 1969, Blass was being transported from Bordeaux Prison for a court hearing at the time of his escape. The escapade was short-lived. Blass was fearless but not too smart: following an anonymous tip, a squad of two hundred armed-to-the-teeth policemen located him a few hours later in his wife's apartment.

Another brief evasion followed in June 1974.

By October of that year, however, he was again on the run, this time having escaped with four others from Saint-Vincent-de-Paul Penitentiary, where he was serving fifteen years for attempted murder, armed robbery, assaulting a policeman, and car theft.

One of Blass's fellow escapees was Jean-Paul Mercier, who, as you will remember, was the good buddy of French gangster Jacques Mesrine. The pair had fled to Venezuela in 1972 after killing two Quebec game wardens, but, with Interpol at their heels, they had parted company. Mesrine went back to his native France, and Mercier returned to Quebec.

Mercier was recaptured in December 1972 and sentenced to life imprisonment for the murder of the game wardens.

"It doesn't matter," he told the court in May 1973, as recorded by *The Globe and Mail* in November 1974. "I'll be out again."

He was as good as his word: over the next year or so, he would again succeed in breaking out of Saint-Vincent-de-Paul — twice. (Ironically, the prison was originally described by its builders as escape-proof.)

Once an escape artist, always an escape artist.

But the clock was ticking down for Mercier. A week after his October 1974 escape in the company of Blass et al., he was wounded in the head and chest during a vicious gunbattle with police, following a bank robbery in Montreal.

"He has found his way out of so many difficult situations," said an SQ spokesman, according to the November 1974 *Globe* article, "and has escaped prison so many times that I wouldn't be shocked if he even cheated death."

Not this time. Mercier died in hospital the following day.

As for Blass, he "celebrated" his freedom in October 1974 by executing two men who had testified against him at his trial in 1969.

Then, in January 1975, with an associate, Blass committed the most odious crime of his short, savage life — the cold-blooded murder in a Montreal nightclub of thirteen people in revenge for the proprietor's possible involvement in a criminal case against Blass's brother. The victims were herded into a storeroom and the place set on fire.

This proved to the swan song for Canada's most wanted killer. Several days later, a team of heavily armed police officers, led by Quebec provincial police detective Albert Lisacek, tracked Blass to a chalet in the Laurentian Mountains and brought him down in a hail of machine-gun fire.

///////////////

After multiple breakouts from Bordeaux in the 1980s and early 1990s, as noted by Bossé and Bouchard, more modern technological measures were put in place to improve surveillance, and escapes, generally, tailed off. The authors reported that the last event of note in the first hundred years of Bordeaux's existence occurred in 2007, when three inmates managed to jump the walls during a major snow storm. They were, however, swiftly recaptured.

But, as in the game of Monopoly, inmates always hope to find that magical get-out-of-jail-free card, and, every so often, they are spectacularly successful.

15

Unlawfully at Large

Walkaways and Mistaken Releases

THE EXPLOITS OF SERIAL ESCAPERS LIKE ERNEST CASHEL AND KEN Leishman and Jean-Paul Mercier and the Stopwatchers pale when compared with those of Ralph Whitfield Morris, who walked away in April 2018 from a minimum-security facility in Mission, BC. Morris was serving a life sentence for the 1982 murder of his intimate partner, Marian Levinski, who had just ended their relationship. And, according to a 2018 *National Post* profile by Joseph Brean, the small, white-haired, eighty-three-year-old Morris, described in a psychologist's report as "a somewhat garrulous, cantankerous, opinionated, self-focused, narcissistic and irritable older inmate," probably held the record for being the target of more police manhunts than anyone else in Canada. Ever.

Morris had threatened, harassed, and stalked Levinski for weeks before confronting her in a bowling alley in Welland, Ontario, and stabbing her to death. At the time, he was on mandatory supervision for an armed robbery conviction, which had earned him an eight-year sentence.

Levinski's death triggered a massive manhunt, the first of many. It was five days before Morris was tracked down to a cottage near Huntsville. He was carrying two rifles, which he dropped when police fired warning shots at him.

But Morris's criminal activities had started way before then. From an early age, as stated in a parole report dated October 27, 2005, there was "a disturbing pattern of violent threatening behaviour involving the use of knives and firearms." He had run away from youth institutions and was considered "delinquent and incorrigible."

His criminal record, described as "lengthy," began in 1951 and consisted initially of crimes against property. His offences took a sinister turn in 1969, when he was convicted of shooting the husband of a woman with whom he was having an affair. Not helpful was the fact that he had long abused valium, alcohol, and other drugs, and that he became addicted to heroin in the late 1990s.

As noted in the parole reports that littered Morris's correctional history, early patterns of hostile behaviour, especially against women, and absconding when frustrated or angry followed him into adulthood. By the early 2000s, he had netted multiple convictions for Escape from Lawful Custody.

While on full parole in 2004, he was accused of assaulting two fellow residents in his low-income housing complex: to wit, he "gouged the eyes" of one resident and challenged another, a senior citizen like himself, to a duel with knives. Police found two knives in his unit that matched the description given by the terrified victim of his bullying. Morris also smelled strongly of booze and appeared to be intoxicated. At the ensuing parole hearing, officers noted that he invariably refused to take responsibility for his actions; rather, he cast himself as the victim. For example, he accused one of the elderly targets of his abuse of teasing him and whistling at him. The board was both unconvinced and unsympathetic, and his parole was revoked.

Even his family was not exempt from his wrath. While unlawfully at large for a two-month period in 2006, he sent threatening letters to his sister and an uncle. Both of them, traumatized, asked for police protection. On being recaptured, Morris claimed that he meant no harm to either of them. He also suggested that his sister's letter of complaint had not been written by her, but that the "parole office had something to do with its composition."

In April 2008, Morris, then seventy-three years old, walked out of a minimum-security Indigenous healing centre at Agassiz, BC, apparently frustrated with all the paperwork required to obtain a transfer to a different facility. Two days later, worn down by the brutal weather conditions, he walked back in.

This walkaway, together with the escape of another dangerous offender from a minimum-security facility, launched a firestorm of criticism against the system that housed inmates with violent records in insecure facilities, with members of the newly elected Conservative federal government and the newly deposed Liberals lobbing verbal grenades at one another.

"We have begun to repair a failed Liberal corrections system," observed a spokesperson for "concerned" Public Safety Minister Stockwell Day in a May 2008 *Globe and Mail* article. Liberal Public Safety critic Ujjal Dosanjh accused Correctional Service Canada (CSC) of a "weak and irresponsible approach" to dealing with such cases. Much tougher rules regarding the assessment of inmates were required.

In the same article, criminology professor Neil Boyd of Simon Fraser University cautioned against jumping to conclusions about failures in the system. Boyd noted that it was not uncommon for convicted murderers to be reintegrated into society, with a stay in a minimum-security facility being one of the final steps in the process. Furthermore, he said, "people can commit pretty violent crimes when they're younger, but the best evidence suggests that no matter what we do, the overwhelming majority age out of crime."

Morris's unlawful exit from the Mission Minimum Institution in April 2018 was short-lived. Staff noticed that he was missing during the 11:00 a.m. count; he was recaptured at about 5:30 p.m. the same day.

This would be the last time Morris would walk out of jail, an unfree man.

In June 2018, just two months later, CSC published a brief news release, advising the public that "on June 22, 2018, Ralph Whitfield MORRIS, an inmate from Mission Institution died while in our custody. At the time of his death, Mr. MORRIS, 83 years old, had been serving an indeterminate sentence for Armed Robbery, Second Degree Murder, Escape Lawful Custody (x3), and Utter Threats to Cause Death/Harm since August 20, 1975."

The fact that inmates like Morris are able to stroll out of jail, seemingly on a whim, remains of great concern to governments, correctional authorities, the police, and the public. What is even more worrying is when an improper or mistaken release helps them along their way.

This is a problem common to all jurisdictions, worldwide. To quote just a few examples: in Britain, close to two hundred mistaken releases were recorded between 2005 and 2009. In the United States, the Department of Justice Office of the Inspector General reported that between 2009 and 2014, staff error had led to 157 "untimely" releases of inmates from federal prisons. A far greater number of releases — 4,183 in all — were classified as untimely for other reasons. And in a report tabled in late 2016, the state auditor-general of Queensland, Australia, revealed that corrective services had committed "frequent" and "significant" errors between 2004 and 2016, leading to the mistaken release of more than ninety prisoners. The mistakes were attributed to communication issues, poor data entry, and the incorrect calculation of sentences.

The problem is widespread in Canada, too.

"Nearly 150 prisoners mistakenly released," announced a headline in *The Toronto Star* in August 2010. According to reporter Daniel Dale, the paper had just received a bundle of 143 heavily censored reports relating to correctional institutions in Ontario for the period between January 2003 and March 2009.

Were any of the walkaways still at large? Were any of them dangerous? Were there any young offenders in the mix? Which facilities were they released from? "This information is not readily available," was the unhelpful response Dale received from Ontario's Ministry of Community Safety and Correctional Services.

The ministry did conceded that "one improper release is one too many." However, according to spokesperson Tony Brown, given that Ontario's thirty-one correctional institutions released about seventy thousand people a year, the percentage of mistaken releases was "infinitesimal." This was scant consolation for someone like Heather Dennie, whose former boyfriend was discharged in error from the Ottawa-Carleton Detention Centre in 2008 and recaptured only six months later. Before his release, he had called Dennie from jail, threatening to kill her.

Generally, according to the ministry, mistakes occurred "as a result of human error, technical error or where an inmate manages to assume the identity of another." In several cases, an inmate was mistakenly set free instead of another who should rightfully have been discharged. Others were sent away because corrections staff misread documents. Some individuals were released on bail even though it had been denied, revoked, or not paid. But the details were meagre and frustratingly vague.

Quebec, too, has had its share of problems, as evidenced in a front-page article by Frédérik-Xavier Duhamel of *The Globe and Mail* in July 2023 entitled "More than 200 Quebec jail inmates freed by mistake since 2015, documents show." Courtesy of the Quebec Ministry of Public Security, the *Globe* had mistakenly received a whopping 384 pages of unredacted incident reports. On discovering its error, the ministry hastily asked the newspaper to destroy the originals and replaced them with redacted versions.

Contrary to the Ontario reports, these documents were astonishingly rich in detail. With or without redactions, they revealed glaring holes in the Quebec correctional system, with police, court officials, and corrections staff all contributing to the chaos. Although most of those released prematurely were rearrested within a few hours, it sometimes took days or even months for mistakes to be rectified. Often, the contact details for offenders or their relatives were incorrect. In some cases, the miscreant was still at large when the report was filed.

Given that many of those let loose were violent criminals, these egregious flaws in the system raised some serious red flags.

The reams of information also showed officials struggling to keep up with their workload. One report, as revealed in the *Globe* article, noted that

"191 emails, totalling 267 documents, were processed on Oct. 25, 2021, by the three sentences [sic] management officers." This e-barrage contributed to the erroneous release of an offender. In another case, a detainee was turned loose prematurely when "a recurring problem with the Outlook messaging system" led to a four-hour delay in the delivery of critical documents.

To protect the privacy of individuals mentioned in the reports, the *Globe* decided not to publish their names. With one exception: Goi Hing Leung, the accused in a 2015 case that received intense public attention at the time.

In November of that year, a homeless man was brutally pummelled with what a police spokesman called "a blunt object," probably a rock, and left bleeding in an alleyway in Montreal's Chinatown. As fifty-year-old Patrick François hovered between life and death in hospital, his two assailants, Goi Hing Leung, forty-two, and Donovan Fisher, nineteen, were arrested and charged with attempted murder. In March 2017, while awaiting trial at Bordeaux Prison (officially the Montreal Detention Centre), Goi was inexplicably handed a release warrant in his name and set free.

The man himself voiced his dismay at being shown the door, but, despite his best efforts — as well as those of his lawyer and representatives of the Crown — prison officials flatly refused to take him back. They relented some ten days after his release upon being ordered to do so by a judge. Goi received a proverbial pat on the back for his honesty. He was not, however, granted bail pending trial, and he was later found guilty of attempted murder.

Another escape from Bordeaux Prison, this one in 2015, was also noted in the *Globe* article.

The mind-boggling details of this incident were widely publicized at the time. On the morning of March 23, 2015, a man named Boucher scrawled his signature onto a form to confirm that his personal effects (identity documents, wallet, lottery ticket, cell phone, eraser, and change) had been returned to him and walked out the door. Problem was, the Boucher who signed for those possessions and nonchalantly left the precinct was not Michel Stéphane Boucher, forty-nine, who was legitimately due for release after two days in detention, but Francis Boucher, thirty-nine, who bore not the slightest resemblance to his namesake, and who was currently partway through a 117-day sentence for having uttered death threats against police officers.

Now, Francis Boucher was not exactly unknown in correctional circles. He was a former member of the defunct Rockers biker gang, which had been affiliated to the notorious Hells Angels, and he had previously served ten years for gangsterism, conspiracy to commit murder, and drug trafficking. His current arrest had stemmed from a drunken incident at a Montreal bar. Then there was Francis's even more famous dad, organized-crime boss and former Hells Angels leader Maurice "Mom" Boucher, who had been found guilty in 2002 of shooting two prison guards to death and was serving consecutive life sentences at the federal penitentiary in Sainte-Anne-des-Plaines, Quebec.

Was Francis Boucher's outrageous discharge an administrative faux pas, an inside job, or something else? The various stakeholders scrambled to find an appropriate answer. According to a *Toronto Star* article on March 24, Marc Lyrette, deputy director of the correctional system in Montreal, put it down to "an administrative error." Quebec Public Security Minister Lise Theriault declared that it was the result of a "stratagem." A spokesperson for the Public Security Department blamed it on a "trick." A day or two later, Boucher's lawyer, Dimitrios Strapatsas, offered his own explanation to CBC News: "After speaking with him, I'm convinced more than ever this was a mistake."

Whatever the reason, the correctional officer who signed the papers should have prevented the error by comparing signatures or checking photo ID. Should have, could have, but did not. Pending an investigation, the man was suspended with pay.

Within days, Boucher was back in jail. He was accused of escaping lawful custody, being at large without lawful excuse, and fraudulent impersonation. At his trial in June 2015, he pleaded guilty to being unlawfully at large. The other charges were dropped, and he received a sixty-day sentence.

Following Boucher's early departure from prison, Public Security Minister Theriault was quoted in the *Star* report as saying that she was looking to tighten security measures at facilities, including biometric identification systems. Clearly, those strategies were either not implemented or were not working. Because just two years later, as per the *Globe*, Goi Hing Leung's release from custody was described by Crown prosecutor Delphine Mauger, once again, as "a major administrative error."

It would seem, as underscored by that treasure trove of 384 pages of criminal incident reports obtained by the *Globe*, that there is still much work to be done when it comes to keeping prisoners behind bars. Because as long as a convincing enough motivation exists or an opportunity presents itself, detainees of all stripes will continue to climb fences or walls, leap out of vehicles, or simply, with or without correctional assistance, stroll away to freedom.

16

With a Little Help

Omid Tahvili, Rabih Alkhalil, and the Leaky North Fraser Pretrial Centre

SECURITY CAMERAS CAPTURE THE TWO MEN WALKING TOWARD A janitor's closet. One of them, wearing red prison-issue T-shirt and pants and with his face hidden by a baseball cap, goes inside, emerging a few minutes later (reminiscent of Clark Kent changing into Superman in the ubiquitous phone booth) in a cleaner's uniform — dark cargo pants and a black golf shirt bearing the cleaning company's logo. The other man, clearly identifiable as a guard, shepherds his companion through several locked doors, including a "mantrap" or double set of doors with a small space between, where the first set must close before the second one can open. At one point, the two men cross paths with another correctional officer. Both "janitor" and guard leave the prison building. Seven minutes later, just one of them — the guard — returns.

The surveillance video of Omid Tahvili's escape from the North Fraser Pretrial Centre (NFPC) in Port Coquitlam, British Columbia, was shot at around 11:30 p.m. on November 14, 2007. In spite of three regular inmate checks by corrections officers and a fourth by a supervisor, it would take nearly twenty-two hours before his absence was noticed. It might conceivably have taken even longer if Tahvili's puzzled cellmate hadn't asked where his roomie had got to.

In a belated attempt to lock the stable door after the horse had bolted, the Coquitlam RCMP sent out an alert to other police agencies in BC, as well as notifying local airports, Canadian Border Services, and United States authorities.

On November 18, *The Province* offered its readers a description of the wanted man: thirty-seven years old; of medium build with black hair and brown eyes; five feet nine inches tall; and weighing 175 pounds. There was a long surgical scar on his abdomen. Quite commonplace so far. Much more useful was that he also had numerous tattoos, including a Celtic cross on his upper back, a tribal tattoo on his right shoulder, and a child's face on each of his upper arms (possibly images of his two children).

"He could be anywhere," RCMP Corporal Tony Farahbakhchian told *The Province*, adding that Tahvili was very much at home in places as far flung as Scotland, Iran, and the United States. In addition: "This guy has a lot of money, so money is not a concern for him. He's a very smart guy, too."

Tahvili always seems to have been smart. *The Province* noted that after immigrating to Canada from Iran in 1994, Tahvili rapidly progressed from working as a dishwasher, bartender, car salesman, and house painter to launching a company called A. and R. Rent a Benz Ltd. a year or so later.

But this should not be seen as an inspiring tale of a self-made man pulling himself up by the bootstraps — Tahvili's money did not come from legitimate sources. Quite the contrary: *Forbes* magazine once described him as "the kingpin of a Persian organized-crime family in Canada connected to various Triads and other global criminal groups."

By 2005, he and his brother-in-law, Royhit Alvin Pal, were in custody, charged with the kidnapping and torture of a Surrey, BC, man. This individual had the misfortune of being related to someone they believed could provide information on the location of $340,000's worth of drug-trafficking spoils. Tahvili was also charged with unlawful confinement, use of an imitation firearm, assault causing bodily harm, sexual assault, and uttering threats. Then there was the little matter of a package seized in 2005 that contained nearly $200,000 in cash. That led to another charge of possession of property obtained from the commission of an indictable offence. Pal was acquitted, but, in October 2007, Tahvili was found guilty of all charges except unlawful confinement and was imprisoned at the NFPC to await his sentence.

Tahvili's nefarious activities were not limited to Canada, however. He was also wanted by U.S. authorities for running a Vancouver-based telemarketing scheme between March 1999 and May 2002, which scammed some US$3 million, mainly from elderly Americans. Victims were conned into believing they could win a lottery if they paid a fee in advance. The Canadian Federal Department of Justice was considering a request to extradite him to face the U.S. charges.

Photograph of Omid Tahvili released by the United States Federal Bureau of Investigation (FBI) in 2005. In addition to charges such as kidnapping and assault in Canada, Tahvili was wanted by the FBI for a telemarketing scam targeting U.S. seniors.

In a *Vancouver Sun* article on November 17, 2007, reporter Kim Bolan marvelled at the ease with which a high-profile inmate like Tahvili could simply saunter away from the fortress-like maximum-security NFPC. The $49-million facility, which opened in 2001, was designed for 490 inmates but was currently housing (and double bunking) 630. A BC Corrections spokesperson insisted that it was one of the most secure prisons in the province, surrounded by high barbed-wire fences and bristling with security cameras and other high-tech devices.

In the final analysis, it all came down to dollars and cents.

As the cynical old saying goes, "Everyone has their price." According to information provided by Tahvili's lawyer, Ron Coumont, at a court hearing in December 2007 — where it was decided to sentence Tahvili in absentia on six charges relating to the violent 2005 kidnapping, assault, and sexual assault — Edwin Ticne's price was $50,000. This, it seems, was what the rogue NFPC guard was promised for helping the convicted Persian gangster to escape.

But, perhaps unsurprisingly, when Ticne went to the prearranged spot to collect the payoff, nobody showed up with the cash. Coumont also informed the court that thirty-five-year-old Ticne had been suspended three times in the previous year. He had both gambling and marital problems. In short, his integrity was questionable.

Generally, the law frowns on people who help people escape from prison. To illustrate, Section 147 of the Canadian Criminal Code in force at the time stated that

Every one who:
a. rescues any person from lawful custody or assists any person in escaping or attempting to escape from lawful custody,
b. being a peace officer, wilfully permits a person in his lawful custody to escape, or
c. being an officer of or an employee in a prison, wilfully permits a person to escape from lawful custody therein, is guilty of an indictable offence and liable to imprisonment for a term not exceeding five years.

Ticne, a correctional officer with ten years' experience, falls neatly into category (c). For his pains, he ended up being charged with permitting a person to escape from lawful custody and obstruction of justice.

Prior to being sentenced in August 2008, as *Northern Daily* informed its readers, Ticne was contrite. "My failure to perform my public duties brought shame and disgrace on myself and my loved ones," he told the court, adding, "I allowed my inner conflicts to consume my better judgment. I have no excuse and I am now prepared to pay my debt to the community."

His "sincerest apology" did not dissuade the judge from deciding that Ticne's debt to the community should consist of thirty-nine months in jail. And, *Northern Daily* added, Crown counsel at the trial conceded that it was unlikely that anyone would ever see or hear from the wealthy gangster again.

Lawyer Coumont shared that opinion. Tahvili had contacted him on several occasions to express appreciation for services rendered. As noted in *News Leader* in December 2007, "I advised him, as an officer of the court, that he should turn himself in. But I don't think he will."

In 2008, a sprinkling of news outlets carried the report that Omid Tahvili, the man who *America's Most Wanted* had breathlessly dubbed "the Tony Soprano of Vancouver," was lying dead somewhere. As *The Vancouver Sun* put it on September 10: "An anonymous tipster has called Coquitlam RCMP Cpl. Scott Baker twice, saying he has the bullet-riddled body of [the] escaped gangster in his refrigerator and wants to trade it for cash. The call is from a phone number in Ontario."

Was this a hoax, perhaps even pulled by Tahvili himself in an attempt to convince the authorities that he was dead? The RCMP were not persuaded that someone, somewhere, had Tahvili on ice. A spokesperson stated that although the Mounties were investigating the tip, they believed that reports of Tahvili's death were "unsubstantiated and unfounded."

///////////////

When Greek police checked the documents of a man pulled over for a traffic violation in 2013, they found that they had snagged a *very* big fish — Rabih Alkhalil, a person of great interest to Canadian authorities.

Alkhalil was wanted in Canada in connection with two high-profile murders.

The first of these was the brazen gangland-style takedown in January 2012 of Sandip Singh Duhre, a Vancouver-area drug lord, in what police believed was a contract killing. Shockingly, the murder took place in a bustling restaurant at the downtown Sheraton Vancouver Wall Centre. Although Alkhalil was not regarded as having pulled the trigger, he had been spotted at the time in the restaurant's bar, and police suspected him of hiring a hitman to take out his major rival. Five months later and halfway across the country, football fan and cocaine dealer Johnny Raposo was also the target of a contract slaying, gunned down at point-blank range as he watched a Eurocup soccer match on the patio of a busy café in Toronto's Little Italy. Again, Alkhalil was implicated, but by the time police got round to raiding his snazzy penthouse in Montreal, he had vanished — only to end up, to their great satisfaction, in the clutches of their Greek counterparts.

Alkhalil, born in 1987, was the youngest of five lawbreaking brothers, two of whom were murdered in gang-related incidents in BC in the early 2000s, and a third shot dead in Mexico in 2018. Rabih was described by investigators as a "Middle Eastern man" of small to medium build, five-foot-ten-inches tall, and weighing around 165 pounds. He had dark brown eyes, black hair, two birthmarks on his left cheek, and a faint scar above his nose. He was a man of many aliases (Rabi, Robby, Robbi, Rabih Al Khalil, Philip Betencourt Furtado, and Philip Bettenecourt Furtado), as well as the owner of multiple fake passports and identity documents. He was also a leader of a Canadian organized-crime group called the Wolfpack Alliance. Cocaine smuggling was one of the Wolfpack's specialties; getting rid of rivals was another.

Extradited back to Canada, Alkhalil, together with three accomplices, faced a first-degree murder charge for Raposo's execution in Little Italy. At Alkhalil's trial in Toronto in 2017, the judge described his attitude as "appalling," with particular reference to his jokey texts to the hitman he had hired for $100,000 to carry out the job, whom he referred to as his "best hitter." Alkhalil was sentenced to life in prison with no chance of parole for twenty-five years, with a concurrent sentence of twenty years for conspiracy to commit the same crime.

Next stop for Alkhalil was Montreal, where, despite legal protests, he was held in the maximum-security wing of the Montreal Detention Centre during his trial for cocaine importing and trafficking. At the time, as reported by Kim Bolan in *The Vancouver Sun* in December 2022, a Quebec judge noted that Quebec's Public Security Ministry had "recommended that he should be held in restrictive conditions and sent to a restrictive unit," adding that "Alkhalil is associated with high level organized crime; he represents a significant flight risk; his security could be compromised because of possible antagonisms." Alkhalil was convicted in 2020 and sentenced to a term of eight years.

Finally, Alkhalil was sent off to Vancouver to face charges for the Duhre killing, as well as the murder in November 2012 of Duhre's fellow crime boss, Sukh Dhak. The trial began in the BC Supreme Court in Vancouver on June 29, 2021. After numerous delays, it finally started winding down in early July 2022.

Alkhalil had pleaded not guilty. But the Crown presented an extremely strong case, backed up by CCTV footage of the scene of the crime and encrypted BlackBerry messages that incriminated the defendant.

Alkhalil was already facing more than two decades of prison time; he clearly had no desire to wait around for any more bad news. The NFPC had been his home away from home during the trial; on July 21, 2022, he quietly took his leave, clad in a black jumpsuit and high visibility vest. He was not alone. Two accomplices posing as contractors working for a vetted company had used a plasma torch to cut through a grate and free him.

Surveillance video caught the trio leaving the prison in a white Ford Econoline van at 6:48 p.m. It took around twenty minutes for prison staff to notice his absence; they alerted Coquitlam RCMP only at 7:30 p.m. It took nearly four hours for the first public announcement to be issued, with the headline "Police looking for Rabih Alkhalil (Robby) who is Unlawfully at Large."

"I think there were some failures in the response," a senior official told Bolan lamely. "They were slow at the switch to disseminate information, slow at the switch to co-ordinate a response."

And some of the information they did disseminate was false — images of the so-called contractors were actually stock photos taken from the internet. As Constable Deanna Law of the RCMP was quoted as saying in a CBC News report the day after Alkhalil slipped out, "It is believed that the suspects who helped Alkhalil escape bear a close resemblance to the photos they left behind, but those images are not of them."

Former BC solicitor general and public safety minister Kash Heed did not pull his punches. "I have never in my thirty-two years in policing, and my time since policing, seen such an inept investigation on a suspected murderer that has escaped from one of our secure institutions," he told Bob Mackin of BIV News.

What about all the security checks and balances that were supposedly in place?

"For you to get into the facility or anywhere near where some of the prisoners would be, especially some of these high risk prisoners, you will have gone through several surveillance systems or you ought to have gone through several surveillance systems, which would have captured your image," fumed Heed.

Mike Laviolette, formerly with the Ottawa Police, first encountered the Alkhalils round 2014 in Ottawa.

"What really brought the Alkhalil family to prominence was a propensity for violence," he told Bolan.

Laviolette's opinion of Rabih's escape closely echoed RCMP Corporal Tony Farahbakhchian's view of Omid Tahvili's escape back in 2007, when Farahbakhchian noted that meticulous planning, experience in travelling widely, and well-stuffed bank accounts make for a successful scheme.

In Laviolette's words: "[Alkhalil's escape] was obviously a very well-planned operation. So my expectation is that he was out of the country as quick as he was out of the jail. He's already demonstrated that you can go to Europe, you can go to South America, you can go wherever the hell you want because money is no object."

Careful preparation, familiarity with travel, scads of cash: just a few of the striking parallels between Tahvili and Alkhalil.

In addition, both men received active assistance from others to get out of prison — a feat that is often not achieved alone. Tahvili's escape differed from Alhalil's, though, in being an inside job. He hacked it by finding what criminal psychologist Michele Y. Deitch calls "the perfect insider": a vulnerable prison employee plagued with personal problems.

Both men slipped away calmly and quietly. This makes a lot of sense, as it enabled them to put distance between themselves and the institution before the alarm was raised. Besides, contrary to commonly held beliefs, the majority of jailbreaks are accomplished without violence, even when, as with this pair, the escapees have a well-documented "propensity for violence."

Tahvili and Alkhalil were both sentenced in absentia for their crimes. In 2007, Tahvili received eleven years for kidnapping. On August 30, 2022, a month after Alkhalil walked away from the NFPC, a BC Supreme Court jury convicted him of conspiracy and first-degree murder for the slaying of Sandip Duhre. He was also found guilty of conspiring to kill Sukh Dhak.

In 2008, after consultations with law enforcement agencies around the world, *Forbes* placed Tahvili among the world's ten most wanted fugitives. He was on the FBI's white-collar wanted list in 2013 for his telemarketing scam that targeted seniors.

In another parallel between the two men, Rabih Alkhalil achieved top ranking as Canada's most wanted man in December 2022, with a bounty of $250,000 offered for his recapture. In April 2024, the Bolo (Be On The Lookout) Program, described on its website as being "an award-winning breakthrough initiative leveraging social media, technology, and innovative engagement to encourage citizens like you to be on the lookout for Canada's most wanted," published its latest lineup of dangerous fugitives. Alkhalil still featured on the list, with Canada-wide warrants for murder, conspiracy to commit murder, and being unlawfully at large — although he had dropped to number four with a reward of just $100,000 for any information leading to his arrest by the RCMP. Ironically, his last known residence was listed on the Bolo website as North Fraser Pretrial Centre, Port Coquitlam, British Columbia.

But, until further notice, we have to accept that NFPC alumni Tahvili and Alkhalil — possibly with the help of some strategic cosmetic procedures (Alkhalil is known to have already had one round of surgery on his nose), certainly with the help of oodles of money — are hanging out somewhere other than at NFPC. Dubai perhaps, or London, or Paris, or even Toronto.

And what of that most basic litmus test for what constitutes a successful escape: getting out or staying out? Here, it must be said that the NFPC lent wings to a brace of the rarest of birds — inmates who nonchalantly strolled out of the premises and, despite the efforts and extensive resources of law enforcement agencies around the world, are still on the lam.

ACKNOWLEDGEMENTS

MY FIRST BOOK EXPLORED CANADA'S 109-YEAR EXPERIMENT WITH capital punishment. The second one focused on the history of Toronto's infamous Don Jail from its inception to the present day. In a sense this book, with its emphasis on the tension between an assortment of historic and contemporary prisons struggling to keep inmates inside and a passel of escapees hell-bent on freedom, may be regarded as the last of a loose trilogy.

Dundurn Press was instrumental in bringing all three of these works to the page. My thanks go to the team for their enthusiastic reception of *On the Lam* and for so ably shepherding it through the various phases of its development.

Book writing can be a lonely undertaking, so I count myself fortunate to have had the support of a committed circle of family, friends, writers, and subject-matter experts.

For the third time, my trusty collaborators Tuhin Giri and Cathy Landolt were continually on hand with constructive suggestions and concrete contributions. It was Tuhin who came up with the book title; he also reviewed many of the chapters and demonstrated remarkable flair as an indexer. In addition to being my social media guru and inspired webmeister, Cathy provided me with sterling assistance in assembling the portfolio of images that grace the pages of this book. Fellow members of my #9 writing group offered useful advice and criticism — especially valued when deadlines loomed.

Special thanks are due to first readers of the manuscript Michael Leonard, Carolyn Poplak, Richard Poplak, and Medeine Tribinevicius, each of whom brought their own distinctive range of expertise to the task. Thanks, too, to Valda Poplak, who applied her usual meticulous attention to the bibliography. Kathryn Lane was an early and ongoing champion of the book, and Jess Shulman brought her extensive talents as an editor to bear on the final draft of the manuscript.

Notable among the individuals who graciously consented to speak with me about their experiences within the Canadian correctional system were Lee Chapelle, Edward Hertrich, Craig Hillen, and Michael Leonard. Their thoughtful observations served to greatly enhance the narrative. Several of my interviewees asked to remain anonymous, and I have, of course, respected their wishes.

In addition to providing me with newspaper articles and other relevant documents, Patrick Kennedy spoke movingly of his family connections with Kingston Penitentiary, and Steven E. Silver, with his encyclopedic knowledge of Kingston–area prisons and prison escapes, plied me with personal anecdotes and a staggering cache of archival material.

I have many organizations on my "thank you" list too.

I was able to rely on the courteous and professional services of a wide variety of Canadian museums, libraries, archives, and other institutions. From east to west across the country, these included the Provincial Archives of New Brunswick and Science East in New Brunswick; Bibliothèque et Archives nationales du Québec in Montreal; Library and Archives Canada in Ottawa; Kingston Penitentiary Tours; the City of Toronto Archives and the Toronto Public Library; the Ontario Provincial Police and the OPP Museum in Orillia; the University of Manitoba Archives & Special Collections; and Burnaby City Museum and the City of Burnaby Archives in British Columbia. I'd like to single out for special mention Canada's Penitentiary Museum in Kingston and its curator Dave St. Onge. And kudos to the museum's then–assistant curator Cameron Willis, whose generosity in painstakingly providing me with both information and images cannot be overstated.

Finally, a big thank you to my husband, Phillip Poplak, my companion on many research trips both at home and away, and dependable provider of both food and feedback while I worked my way through the book.

BIBLIOGRAPHY

General

Capital Case Files, RG 13, Department of Justice (Canada), Library and Archives Canada, Ottawa.
James, Bill. *Popular Crime: Reflections on the Celebration of Violence.* Scribner, 2011.

Introduction

Culp, Richard F. "Frequency and Characteristics of Prison Escapes in the United States: An Analysis of National Data." *Prison Journal* 85, no. 3 (2005): 270–91.
Duckett, Mona T., and Johann W. Mohr. "Prison." In *The Canadian Encyclopedia*, June 8, 2015. thecanadianencyclopedia.ca/en/article/prison.
Friedland, Martin. *Sentencing Structure in Canada: Historical Perspectives.* Department of Justice Canada, Policy, Programs and Research Branch, Research and Development Directorate: [Ottawa], 1988.
Globe and Mail editions of July 14, 1980; July 26, 1980; August 9, 1980.
Graham, Bob. "Execution Kinder than 'Slow Death,' Lifer Says." *Toronto Star*, February 17, 1981.
Hutchison, Bill. "Hollowed Food Trays Help Inmate Escape Maximum Security." *Kingston Whig-Standard*, May 26, 1980.
Madzharov, Emil. "The Motivation for Escaping from Prisons." *International Scientific Journal: Security & Future* 5, no. 4 (2021): 122–25.
Peterson, Bryce Elling, Adam Fera, and Jeff Mellow. "Escapes from Correctional Custody: A New Examination of an Old Phenomenon." *Prison Journal* 96, no. 4 (2016): 511–33.

1: Dead Man's Trousers

Calgary Daily Herald edition of May 10, 1930.
Calgary Herald editions of January 25, 1904; December 5, 1964.
Evening Journal (Edmonton) edition of January 25, 1904.
Globe editions of October 28, 1903; January 25, 1904; February 3, 1904.
Manitoba Morning Free Press edition of January 25, 1904.
Report of the North-West Mounted Police 1903. S.E. Dawson, 1904.
Vancouver Daily World edition of February 2, 1904.
Weekly Albertan edition of January 28, 1904.
Weekly News Record edition of March 3, 1904.
Wetaskiwin Times edition of August 20, 1925.
Winnipeg Tribune edition of February 2, 1904.

2: Smokescreens

Brown, Jim. *The Golden Boy of Crime: The Almost Certainly True Story of Norman "Red" Ryan.* HarperCollins, 2019.
Butts, Edward. *Line of Fire: Heroism, Tragedy, and Canada's Police.* Dundurn Press, 2009.
"CANADA: Ticket-of-Leave Man." *Time*, June 8, 1936.
Globe editions of September 11, 1923; March 7, 1936; May 25, 1936; May 26, 1936; May 27, 1936.
Honderich, Ted. "Why Red Ryan's Shadow Still Hangs over Every Prison Yard." *Maclean's*, December 7, 1957.
"Kingston Penitentiary: Ernest Hemingway's Story on the Dramatic Jailbreak of 1923." *Toronto Star*, April 20, 2012.
McSherry, Peter. *The Big Red Fox: The Incredible Story of Norman "Red" Ryan, Canada's Most Notorious Criminal.* Dundurn Press, 1999.
Toronto Daily Star editions of July 25, 1935; February 29, 1936; May 26, 1936.

3: Revisiting the Big House

Clark, Robert. *Down Inside: Thirty Years in Canada's Prison Service.* Goose Lane Editions, 2017.
"Craft Takes All Blame for Killing Messenger." *Globe and Mail*, June 19, 1948.

BIBLIOGRAPHY

Curtis, Dennis, Andrew Graham, Lou Kelly, and Anthony Patterson. *Kingston Penitentiary: The First Hundred and Fifty Years, 1835–1985.* Minister of Supply and Services Canada, 1985.
Edmison, J.A. "The History of Kingston Penitentiary." *Historic Kingston, Being the Transactions of the Kingston Historical Society for 1953–54.* Kingston Historical Society, 1954.
Fogarty, Catherine. *Murder on the Inside: The True Story of the Deadly Riot at Kingston Penitentiary.* Biblioasis, 2021.
Globe edition of April 26, 1904.
Globe and Mail editions of April 27, 1948; September 30, 2013.
Gundy, H.P. "Thomson, Hugh Christopher." In *Dictionary of Canadian Biography*, vol. 6. University of Toronto/Université Laval, 2003–. biographi.ca/en/bio/thomson_hugh_christopher_6E.html.
Hennessy, Peter H. *Canada's Big House: The Dark History of the Kingston Penitentiary.* Dundurn Press, 1999.
"Interesting Facts." *Canada's Penitentiary Museum.* Accessed October 3, 2024. penitentiarymuseum.ca/history/interesting-facts/.
Kennedy, Patrick. "The Day They Killed Uncle Johnny." *Kingston Whig-Standard*, April 28, 2012.
MacIntyre, Linden, and Theresa Burke. *Who Killed Ty Conn.* Creative Publishers, 2011.
McSherry, Peter. *What Happened to Mickey?: The Life and Death of Donald "Mickey" McDonald, Public Enemy No. 1.* Dundurn Press, 2013.
Montreal Gazette edition of September 13, 1945.
Parks Canada. *Directory of Federal Heritage Designations: Kingston Penitentiary National Historic Site of Canada.* Accessed October 10, 2024. pc.gc.ca/apps/dfhd/page_nhs_eng.aspx?id=401&i=57117.
Swackhamer, Jason William. *Report of the Commission of Inquiry into Certain Disturbances at Kingston Penitentiary during April, 1971.* Information Canada, 1973.
Vallée, Brian. "Conn Was Inspired by His Hero, Edwin Alonzo Boyd." *Globe and Mail*, May 22, 1999.

4: High Flyer

Brandon Sun edition of September 6, 1966.
Cassidy, Christian. "Kenneth Leishman — The Flying Bandit." *This Was Manitoba* (blog). 2008, 2011. Accessed April 12, 2024. thiswaswinnipeg.blogspot.com/2008/07/flying-bandit.html.
Edmonton Journal editions of March 2, 1966; March 11, 1978.

Globe and Mail editions of May 5, 1966; June 9, 1966; May 8, 1974; December 18, 1980.
Handman, Stanley. "He Went on Business Trips — To Rob Banks." *Ottawa Citizen*, July 18, 1958.
Leader-Post (Regina) editions of March 2, 1966; September 2, 1966; September 27, 1980; January 9, 1982.
Montreal Gazette edition of September 26, 1980.
Ottawa Citizen edition of February 19, 1983.
Robertson, Heather. *The Flying Bandit*. Lorimer, 1981.
Vancouver Sun edition of April 9, 1958.
Windsor Star edition of September 9, 1966.
Winnipeg Sun edition of August 17, 2003.

5: Maximum Security

Caron, Roger. *Go-Boy! This Is the True Story of Life Behind Bars*. Hamlyn Paperbacks, 1979.
Cawley, Laurence. "Where Do Prison Escapees and Absconders Actually Go?" BBC News, February 24, 2017. bbc.com/news/uk-england-39037965.
Correctional Service Canada. "Millhaven Institution." Updated September 12, 2017. canada.ca/en/correctional-service/corporate/facilities-security/institutional-profiles/ontario/millhaven-institution.html.
Fogarty, Catherine. *Murder on the Inside: The True Story of the Deadly Riot at Kingston Penitentiary*. Biblioasis, 2021.
Forestell, Michelle Dorey. "Officer Recalls the Summer of '72 Millhaven Escape." *Kingstonist*, July 10, 2022. kingstonist.com/news/officer-recalls-the-summer-of-72-millhaven-escape/.
Globe and Mail editions of March 23, 1964; July 20, 1971; October 19, 1971; July 12, 1972.
Hamilton Spectator editions of August 25, 1993; October 2, 1993; February 12, 1994.
Kennedy, Patrick. "Family Recounts Brush with Escaped Millhaven Pen Inmate Half a Century Ago." *Kingston Whig-Standard*, July 2, 2022.
Kingston Whig-Standard editions of August 6, 1969; July 11, 1972; July 17, 1972; July 18, 1972; November 30, 1972; June 9, 1978.
Kitchener Waterloo Record edition of October 29, 1981.
Ottawa Citizen editions of July 11, 1972; July 8, 1978; August 1, 1979.
Province edition of August 18, 1972.
Toronto Star editions of April 20, 1971; July 11, 1972.
Vancouver Sun edition of August 17, 1972.

6: A Dog's Life

Berrigan, George T. *Police Stories: Tales from a Small-Town Cop*. Borealis Press, 2008.
Friends of the OPP Museum. "Cloud II. A Hero's Life." *Newsletter, Winter 2012* 5, no. 1 (2012): 1–2. oppmuseumfriends.ca/wp-content/uploads/2019/10/Friends-newsletter-Feb-2012-WEB.pdf.
Globe and Mail editions of August 4, 1975; August 5, 1975; August 6, 1975; August 7, 1975; August 8, 1975; August 9, 1975; August 19, 1975; August 21, 1975; September 2, 1975; September 6, 1975; January 29, 1976; March 18, 1976; April 13, 1976; April 14, 1976; April 16, 1976; April 24, 1976; October 27, 1976; December 1, 1976.
Toronto Star editions of August 4, 1975; August 5, 1975; August 6, 1975; August 7, 1975; August 15, 1975; August 16, 1975; September 2, 1975; September 4, 1975; September 12, 1975; September 18, 1975; September 26, 1975; October 27, 1976.

7: "Le Grand Gangster"

Butts, Edward. *Line of Fire: Heroism, Tragedy, and Canada's Police*. Dundurn Press, 2009.
Calgary Herald edition of November 5, 1979.
Correctional Service Canada. *Commemorative Booklet for the Closing of St. Vincent de Paul Penitentiary 1873–1989*. Accessed October 9, 2024. publicsafety.gc.ca/lbrr/archives/hv%209510.13%205%201873-1989-eng.pdf.
Drouin, Alex. "Testimonies: Police Officers Machine-Gunned by Criminal Jacques Mesrine." *Journal de Montreal*, September 3, 2019.
Globe and Mail editions of September 18, 1969; August 22, 1972; May 14, 1973; June 7, 1973; June 15, 1973; November 2, 1974; May 9, 1978; September 18, 1979; November 3, 1979; November 5, 1979.
Laentz, Michel. *Jacques Mesrine: L'histoire vraie de l'ennemi public no 1*. International Stars Edition, 2012.
Lichfield, John. "Jacques Mesrine: Le Grand Gangster." *Independent*, August 3, 2009.
Mesrine, Jacques. *L'instinct de mort*. Flammarion, 2008.
Montreal Gazette editions of November 3, 1979, November 5, 1979.
Montreal Star editions of August 21, 1972; August 28, 1972.
Spectator edition of August 23, 1972.

Toronto Daily Star editions of July 17, 1969; September 17, 1969; May 14, 1978; November 2, 1979; November 3, 1979.

8: Marking Time

Dean, Josh. "The Life and Times of the Stopwatch Gang." *Atavist Magazine*, no. 46 (2015). magazine.atavist.com/the-life-and-times-of-the-stopwatch-gang/.
Globe and Mail editions of December 16, 1959; August 19, 1961; November 22, 1961; November 14, 1973; March 6, 1975; June 6, 1975; June 11, 1999; January 16, 2007.
Hertrich, Edward. *Wasted Time*. Dundurn Press, 2019.
Kingston Whig-Standard editions of August 24, 1979; February 2, 1994.
Mitchell, Patrick Michael. *This Bank Robber's Life: The Life and Fast Times of Patrick "Paddy" Mitchell*. BookBaby, 2002.
Ottawa Citizen editions of April 18, 1974; November 17, 1979.
Proctor, Jason. "Author and Bank Robber Stephen Reid Dead at Age 68." CBC News, June 13, 2018. cbc.ca/news/canada/british-columbia/stephen-reid-stopwatch-gang-author-obituary-1.4704842.
"Stephen Reid's 10 Toughest Prisons in North America." *Maclean's*, December 27, 2005.
Toronto Daily Star edition of July 25, 1959.
Toronto Star editions of May 29, 1986; January 17, 1988; June 11, 1999.
Weston, Greg. *The Stopwatch Gang*. Macmillan Canada, 1992.

9: Fare and Foul

Globe and Mail editions of November 28, 1958; December 30, 1981; December 1, 1982.
Munch, John. "Don Jail Break Is No Surprise to Guards." *Toronto Star*, December 31, 1981.
Tesher, Ellie. "Don Escapers' Cabby Lives a Year of Horror over Lie." *Toronto Star*, December 23, 1982.
Toronto Star editions of January 25, 1981; March 13, 1981; August 18, 1981; December 26, 1981; December 27, 1981; December 29, 1981; December 30, 1981; January 4, 1982; January 27, 1982; February 10, 1982; September 25, 1982; October 22, 1982; December 1, 1982.

10: There Be Monsters

"Allan Legere's Transfer to Lower Security Raises Fears in Miramichi." CBC News, February 3, 2015. cbc.ca/news/canada/new-brunswick/allan-legere-s-transfer-to-lower-security-raises-fears-in-miramichi-1.2943190.

Appleby, Timothy. "Legere's 'Jekyll-Hyde' Character Fooled Jail Officials, Warden Says." *Globe and Mail*, November 25, 1989.

Butts, Edward. "Allan Legere Case." In *The Canadian Encyclopedia*, September 19, 2017. thecanadianencyclopedia.ca/en/article/allan-legere-case.

Calgary Herald editions of January 14, 1983; October 2, 1999; September 12, 2001; September 14, 2001; October 6, 2001; November 3, 2001.

"Convict's Escape Strictly a Snow Job." *Vancouver Sun*, March 25, 1982.

Cox, Kevin. "DNA Tests Link Legere to Three N.B. Murders: Genetic Fingerprinting Evidence Crucial to Crown's Case." *Globe and Mail*, October 18, 1991.

Cox, Kevin. "Legere Charged with Four Murders: Trial to Be Important Test Case for New Forensic Procedure." *Globe and Mail*, November 21, 1990.

Dolphin, Ric. "Getting Tougher at the Max." *Edmonton Journal*, September 12, 1994.

Edmonton Journal editions of July 8, 1982; April 20, 2009.

Gérard V. La Forest Law Library. Allan Legere Digital Archive. University of New Brunswick. unb.ca/fredericton/law/library/digital-collections/allan-legere/index.html.

Globe and Mail editions of January 10, 1987; January 23, 1987; June 13, 1989; October 17, 1989; October 18, 1989; November 2, 1991; October 31, 2009.

Henton, Darcy. "Sex Killer Harvey Andres Escaped from Edmonton's Max — Twice." *Edmonton Journal*, January 24, 2009.

Jones, Robert. "Suspect in 4 Slayings Has Violent Record." *Globe and Mail*, November 21, 1989.

MacLean, Rick. "Locked-Up Fear Along the Miramichi: LETTER FROM NEWCASTLE, N.B." *Globe and Mail*, November 4, 1989.

Nelson, Chris. "At Least Omar Khadr Got His Day in Court." *Calgary Herald*, June 6, 2013.

Ottawa Citizen editions of November 29, 1976; July 7, 1982.

R v. Andres (H.H), [2003] 339 A.R. 334 (CA).

Slade, Daryl. "Science Solves Johnston Case." *Calgary Herald*, November 3, 2001.

Toronto Star editions of June 18, 1989; October 16, 1989; November 4, 1991.

Tourism New Brunswick. tourismnewbrunswick.ca

Veniot, André. "Allan Legere: A Look Back." Gérard V. La Forest Law Library. Allan Legere Digital Archive. University of New Brunswick. unb.ca/fredericton/law/library/_resources/pdf/legal-materials/allan-legere/comms_bibliography/legere-veniot__allan_joseph_legere__.pdf.

Zinger, Ivan. "Office of the Correctional Investigator 2018–2019 Annual Report." oci-bec.gc.ca/en/content/office-correctional-investigator-annual-report-2018–2019.

11: Porous Walls

Andersen, Earl. *Hard Place to Do Time: The Story of Oakalla Prison, 1912–1991*. Hillpointe Publishing, 1993.

Azpiri, Jon. "How a Bloody Riot and Massive Prison Break Brought Down Oakalla, B.C.'s Most Notorious Jail." Global News, August 31, 2018. globalnews.ca/news/4414861/oakalla-prison-riot-escape/.

Globe and Mail edition of January 5, 1988.

Mason, Brian, Colin J. McMechan, and Catherine M. Angellen, eds. *Corrections in British Columbia: Pre-Confederation to the Millennium*. Justice Institute of British Columbia, Corrections & Community Justice Division, 2003.

Montreal Gazette edition of November 23, 1983.

"The Oakalla Jailbreak." *Maclean's*, January 18, 1988.

"Oakalla Prison." *The Sunday Historian* (blog). December 6, 2020. Accessed May 13, 2023. thesundayhistorian.ca/post/oakalla-prison.

Ottawa Citizen edition of October 3, 1952.

Prince Albert Daily Herald edition of May 27, 1937.

Schaefer, Glen. "Oakalla's Age Considered a Cause of Riots." *Vancouver Sun*, November 23, 1983.

Spokane Chronicle edition of January 4, 1988.

"Summer of Yippie!" *Past Tense: Vancouver Histories* (blog). June 23, 2011. pasttensevancouver.wordpress.com/tag/oakalla/.

Toronto Star edition of January 6, 1988.

Vancouver Sun editions of March 14, 1931; October 23, 1979.

12: "Run, Bambi, Run"

Bembenek, Lawrencia. *Woman on Trial*. HarperCollins, 1992.

Chronicle-Journal (Thunder Bay) edition of January 31, 2016.

Drury, Bob, and Marnie Inskip. "Was Bambi Framed?" *Vanity Fair*, October 1991.
Globe and Mail editions of October 18, 1990; June 15, 1991.
Greenya, John. "Bambi, on the Lam." *Washington Post*, August 22, 1990.
Greenya, John. "Most Wanted 'Bambi' Found." *Washington Post*, October 18, 1990.
Gunn, Erik. "From the Archive: Laurie Bembenek's Last Days." *Milwaukee Magazine*, June 21, 2011.
Hevesi, Dennis. "Lawrencia Bembenek, 'Bambi' in Murder Case, Dies at 52." *New York Times*, November 21, 2010.
Lakey, Jack. "Bambi Behind Bars: An Exclusive Interview." *Toronto Star*, January 27, 1991.
Milwaukee Journal Sentinel editions of November 21, 2010; September 12, 2023.
Radish, Kris. *Run, Bambi, Run: The Beautiful Ex-Cop and Convicted Murderer Who Escaped to Freedom and Won America's Heart*. Birch Lane Press, 1992.
Ramsland, Katherine. "Suspects." TruTV. Accessed October 7, 2023. trutv.com/library/crime/notorious_murders/women/bambenek/4.html.
Toronto Star edition of October 18, 1990.
Walsh, Mary Williams. "COLUMN ONE: Political Prisoner or Killer?" *LA Times*, January 10, 1992.
Washington Post edition of October 18, 1990.
Worthington, Peter. "Bambi Pal Finally Paid Back." *Toronto Sun*, July 9, 1992.
Worthington, Peter. "Clearly Somebody's Lying." *Toronto Sun*, July 24, 1992.
Worthington, Peter. "A New Trial for Bembenek?" *Toronto Sun*, December 1, 1992.
Worthington, Peter. "The Squeezing of Louis Kebezes." *Toronto Sun*, June 30, 1992.

13: Blade Runners

AP News. Accessed March 17, 2024. apnews.com/article/3f5438b065612f72a549cd163fc022d8.
Brean, Joseph. "SWAT Team Arrests Three Quebec Fugitives at Luxury Montreal Condo After Helicopter Jailbreak." *National Post*, January 25, 2015.
CBC News posts of December 20, 2017; February 28, 2018.

Criminal Intelligence Service Canada. *2003 Annual Report on Organized Crime in Canada*. Criminal Intelligence Service Canada, 2004.
CTV News post of March 17, 2013.
France24 post of October 3, 2018.
George, Tosin. "Prison Helicopter Escapes: An Analysis of Prison Escape Attempts from 1971 to 2020." *Tosin George's Blog* (blog). September 21, 2022. tosingeorge.hashnode.dev/prison-helicopter-escapes-analysis.
Globe and Mail editions of May 8, 1981; June 19, 1990; August 2, 1990.
Guardian editions of July 1, 2018; October 26, 2023.
Ha, Tu Thanh. "A History of Brazen Acts: Behind the Chopper Jail Break." *Globe and Mail*, November 3, 2014.
Honolulu Advertiser edition of May 9, 1981.
Independent edition of April 18, 2013.
Koetsier, John. "Global First: Autonomous Drone Gets Approval to Fly with Passengers." *Forbes*, October 13, 2023.
LA Times edition of May 27, 1986.
Leitenyi, Patrick. "How the Hells Angels Conquered Canada." *Vice*, October 27, 2016.
Montreal Gazette editions of May 8, 1981; March 19, 2013; November 25, 2015; May 17, 2023.
Paris Match edition of September 28, 2018.
Peritz, Ingrid. "Police Warned Prison Guards of Possible Escape Attempt." *Globe and Mail*, June 17, 2014.
Perreaux, Les, and Tu Thanh Ha. "Jailbreak: A Tense Collision of Fear and Flying." *Globe and Mail*, March 19, 2013.
Picard, André. "Massive Manhunt Under Way." *Globe and Mail*, June 9, 2014.
Quan, Douglas. "Chopper Incident Stirs Dark Memories for Pilot." *Montreal Gazette*, June 12, 2014.
"St. Jérôme: Évasion en hélicoptère caméra 1." *Journal de Montreal* video, 6:01. March 14, 2016. journaldemontreal.com/2016/03/14/leur-evasion-en-helico-a-pris-six-longues-minutes.
Toronto Star edition of April 27, 2024.
"Video of Helicopter Escape from St-Jérôme Jail Made Public." CBC News, March 15, 2016. cbc.ca/news/canada/montreal/video-helicopter-jail-escape-1.3492898.
Willsher, Kim. "'Gun to Head': French Prison Break Helicopter Pilot Describes Ordeal." *Guardian*, July 5, 2018.
Yan, Holly. "Canadian Prisoners Captured After Daring Helicopter Escape." CNN, March 18, 2013. cnn.com/2013/03/18/world/americas/canada-prison-escape/.

14: Island Retreat

Bossé, Sébastien, and Chantal Bouchard. *Bordeaux: L'histoire d'une prison.* Les Éditions au Carré, 2013.
Carle, Paul. "The Ultimate Report by Jean-Patrice Desjardins: Richard Blass in Val-David." *L'Histoire de Val-David.* Accessed July 29, 2023. histoirevaldavid.com/le-reportage-ultime-de-jean-patrice-desjardins-richard-blass-a-val-david/.
Dorion, Frederic. *Special Public Inquiry 1964 — Report of the Commissioner, the Honourable Frederic Dorion, Chief Justice of the Superior Court for the Province of Quebec.* Privy Council Office, 1965.
Globe and Mail editions of March 4, 1965; July 17, 1965; April 20, 1967; November 2, 1974.
Ha, Tu Thanh. "Montreal Mobster Nearly Sank Liberals." *Globe and Mail,* February 14, 2002.
"History Through Our Eyes: March 4, 1965, Lucien Rivard Escapes." *Montreal Gazette,* March 4, 2019.
Montreal Gazette editions of March 4, 1965; June 5, 1965; July 17, 1965.
Pape, Gordon. "Rivard Letter — Laughs for House." *Montreal Gazette,* March 5, 1965.

15: Unlawfully at Large

Brean, Joseph. "'Cantankerous' Murder Convict, 83, Adds to Long String of Escapes by Walking from B.C. Minimum Security Prison." *National Post,* May 3, 2018.
Briggs, Casey. "More than 90 Queensland Prisoners Mistakenly Released Early, Report Finds." ABC News, November 29, 2016. abc.net.au/news/2016-11-29/more-than-90-qld-prisoners-mistakenly-released-too-early/8075886.
Canadian Press. "Dangerous Biker Francis Boucher Mistakenly Released from Jail After Threatening to Kill Police Officer." *National Post,* March 24, 2015.
Dale, Daniel. "Nearly 150 Prisoners Mistakenly Released." *Toronto Star,* August 24, 2010.
Duhamel, Frédérik-Xavier. "More than 200 Quebec Jail Inmates Freed by Mistake Since 2015, Documents Show." *Globe and Mail,* July 20, 2023.
"Francis Boucher, 'Mom' Boucher's Son, Pleads Guilty After Wrongful Jail Release." CBC News, June 10, 2015. cbc.ca/news/canada/montreal

/francis-boucher-mom-boucher-s-son-pleads-guilty-after-wrongful-jail
-release-1.3107950.

"Francis Boucher, Son of Hells Angels Kingpin, Charged After Surrendering." CBC News, March 27, 2015. cbc.ca/news/canada/montreal/francis-boucher-son-of-hells-angels-kingpin-charged-after-surrendering-1.3011755.

Globe and Mail edition of January 25, 1975.

Government of Canada National Parole Board. "NPB Release Decision Sheets." cbc.ca/bc/news/bc-080430-morris-parole-documents.pdf.

Hristova, Bobby. "11 Inmates Mistakenly Released from Hamilton Jail Since 2021, Documents Show." CBC News, July 31, 2023. cbc.ca/news/canada/hamilton/hamilton-inmates-mistakenly-released-1.6920277.

Journal de Montreal editions of March 27, 2015; November 23, 2015; April 16, 2017.

Keller, James. "Convicted Killer Returns to B.C. Prison." *Globe and Mail*, May 2, 2008.

Montreal Gazette edition of November 24, 2015.

Office of the Inspector General U.S. Department of Justice. "DOJ OIG Releases Report on Untimely Releases of Inmates from Federal Prisons." May 24, 2016. oig.justice.gov/sites/default/files/2019-12/2016-05-24.pdf.

Toronto Star edition of March 24, 2015.

16: With a Little Help

Bolan, Kim. "Gangster's Escape Raises Concerns About Jail Security." *Vancouver Sun*, December 12, 2022.

Bolo Program: Canada's 25 Most Wanted. boloprogram.org/.

Brown, Robert. "America's Most Wanted: Omid Tahvili." *America's Most Wanted*, January 2, 2008.

CBC News post of July 23, 2022.

Colebourn, John. "Suspect in Gangland Killing Caught in Greece Traffic Stop." *Province*, May 2, 2013.

CP24 post of July 23, 2022.

Criminal Code, R.S.C., 1985, c. C-46.

Hall, Neal. "Guard Led Prisoner in Jail Escape, Video Shows." *Vancouver Sun*, December 5, 2007.

Knox, Jules, and Elizabeth Sargeant. "Most Wanted: Rabih Alkhalil, Convicted for Two Murders, Wanted for a Jailbreak." Global News, November 17, 2023. globalnews.ca/news/10096263/crime-beat-most-wanted-rabih-alkhalil/.

Mackin, Bob. "Full Investigation of Rabih Alkhalil Escape Needed, Say Those Familiar with North Fraser Pretrial Centre." BIV, July 26, 2022. biv.com/news/economy-law-politics/full-investigation-rabih-alkhalil-escape-needed-say-those-familiar-north-fraser-8268539.

News Leader edition of December 8, 2007.

Northern Daily edition of August 12, 2008.

Payne, Sarah. "Burnaby Guard Never Got His Payoff: Lawyer." *News Leader*, December 8, 2007.

Province editions of November 19, 2007; December 11, 2007.

Saltman, Jennifer. "Gangster Escapes from Jail." *Province*, November 18, 2007.

Toronto Sun edition of June 14, 2017.

Tri-City News editions of April 6, 2008; September 10, 2008.

Vancouver Sun editions of November 17, 2007; December 5, 2007; September 10, 2008; July 6, 2022; July 23, 2022; December 7, 2022.

Vardi, Nathan. "In Pictures: The World's 10 Most Wanted Fugitives. *Forbes*, May 13, 2010.

IMAGE CREDITS

12	Photographer unknown. Public domain.
25	*Globe* edition of May 25, 1936.
26	*Globe* staff photos. *Globe* edition of May 25, 1936.
31	Canada's Penitentiary Museum.
33	Canada's Penitentiary Museum, accession number 6765.
34	Canada's Penitentiary Museum, accession number 8213.
35	Canada's Penitentiary Museum, accession number 8929.
39	Photograph by Meyers Studios. Canada's Penitentiary Museum, accession number 2023.051S.
52	The University of Manitoba Archives & Special Collections, *The Winnipeg Tribune* Photograph Collection, PC 18, item# UM_pc018_A81-012_031_1794_082_0001.
60	Canada's Penitentiary Museum.
76	Image courtesy of The OPP Museum.
85	Photograph by author.
100	*The Kingston Whig-Standard*, a division of Postmedia Network Inc.
107	City of Toronto Archives, Fonds 2032, Series 841, File 24, Item 1.
120	The Provincial Archives of New Brunswick, item number P194-1322.
127	City of Burnaby Archives, Paul Norton. Photo ID 556-549.
135	City of Burnaby Archives, Paul Norton. Photo ID 556-552.
144	*The Toronto Sun*, a division of Postmedia Network Inc. Reproduced with permission.
149	Photograph by Adrian Pingstone. Public domain.
161	Photographer unknown. BAnQ Vieux-Montréal, La Presse fonds, (06M,P833,S3,D796). Public domain.
179	FBI Crime Alert. Public domain.

INDEX

Italicized locators refer to illustrations.

Abrams, Frank, 110, 113
ADX Florence, 88
Air Canada, 48, 51, 96, 97
Alcatraz (U.S. Penitentiary), 94
Alkhalil, Rabih "Robby," 181–86
Alouette II (helicopter), 155, 156
America's Most Wanted, 102, 142, 181
Andersen, Earl, 126, 131, 133
Andres, Harvey Harold, 121–24
Anthracite (North-West Territories, now Alberta), 8
AP News, 154
Archambault Institution, 84
Arizona State Penitentiary, 102
Atavist Magazine, 98, 102
Atlantic Institution, 116–17

Babcock, William, 130
Backlin, Harry, 48
Baker, Shirley Ann, 121, 123
Bambi. *See* Bembenek, Lawrencia "Laurie" Ann
Barnett, Cunliffe, 131
Bath Institution, 1, 58
BC Supreme Court, 183
BCTV, 133
Beaupré, Roger, 162
Belgrade (Yugoslavia, now Serbia), 67–68
Bell 206 (helicopter), 154
Bell, Don, 111
Belt, Isaac Rufus, 7, 9, 14–15
Bembenek, Lawrencia "Laurie" Ann, 4, 138–43, *144*, 145–46
Bennett, R. B., 21–22, 27
Berrigan, George, 77
Berthomet, Stéphane, 153
Besse, François, 89
Big Red Fox, The (McSherry), 18, 27
BIV News, 184

Blass, Richard "Le Chat," 3, 165–66
Blyth (Constable), 9
Bolan, Kim, 180, 183
Bolo Program, 185
Book of Lists, The, 93
Boomer, Charles Warren "The Satchel Bandit," 66–68
Bordeaux (Bossé and Bouchard), 160
Bordeaux Prison, 159–60, *161*, 164, 166,
    capital punishment and, 161–62
    escapes from, 162, 165, 167
    mistaken releases from, 174–75
Bossé, Sébastien, 160, 166
Bouchard, Chantal, 160, 166
Boucher, Francis, 174–75
Boucher, Maurice "Mom," 175
Boucher, Michel Stéphane, 174
Bourgeois, Jacques, 163
Boyd, Edwin Alonzo, 41
Boyd, Neal, 171
Boyd Gang, 36, 107
Brandon Sun (newspaper), 51
Brean, Joseph, 169
Brewster, William, 127
British Broadcasting Corporation (BBC), 68
British Columbia Penitentiary, 127
Bryans, Thomas, 17
Burke, Theresa, 41
Burnaby (British Columbia), 125–26, 128, 134
Burton (New Brunswick), 119
Bush, Brian William, 109–12
Butner (North Carolina), 103
butter, 4, 36
Butts, Edward, 86

Cadeddu, Frederick Fernando "Foxy Freddie," 1, 4

Calgary (Alberta), 9, 11, 13, 15, 121, 122–23
Calgary Daily Herald, 8, 10
Calgary Herald, 14, 122, 123
Campbell, Vernon "Blackie," 128–29
Canada's Penitentiary Museum, 5, 32, 58
Canadian Broadcasting Corporation (CBC), 41, 104, 120
Canadian Crime Stoppers Association, 117
Canadian Criminal Code, 180
Canadian Federal Department of Justice, 179
Canadian Forces (military), 54, 63, 66
Canadian Justice for Animals in Service Act, 77
Canadian Mounted Rifles, 13
Canadian Penitentiary Service, 53
capital punishment, 2, 9–10, 40
    death cell and watch, 10, 106
    hangman, 14–15, 130, 161
Caron, Roger, 57, 59
Carson, Raymond, 65, 74–75, *76*, 79
Cashel, Ernest, 7–11, *12*, 13–15, 169
Cashel, John, 10, 14
CBC News, 148, 175, 184. *See also* Canadian Broadcasting Corporation.
Chatham Head (New Brunswick), 115–18
Checkley, Harry, 25
Chertsey (Quebec), 150
Chronicle-Journal, 145
Clark, Donald, 61
Clark, Robert, 42
Clarke, Roy "Binky," 37
Cloud II, 65–66, 74–75, *76*, 77–79
CNN, 152, 155
Coffin, Wilbert, 162
Collins Bay Institution, 58, 62, 99
Columbia Grill & Tavern (Thunder Bay, Ontario), 137, 142
Conn, Tyrone Williams "Ty," 40–42
Correctional Service Canada (CSC), 42, 59, 171–72
Corrections in British Columbia, 125
Corrigan, Derek, 134
Côté, Médéric, 87
Coughlan, D. W. F., 28

Couillard, Philippe, 153
Coumont, Ron, 180
Coutanche, Gary, 96–97
Craft, Austin, 37
Criminal Intelligence Service Canada, 148
Culp, Richard, 3

Daily British Whig, 30
Dale, Daniel, 172
Dale, Joseph William, 49, 51
Daudet, Léon, 88
Daughney, Donna, 117
Daughney, Linda, 117
Dean, Josh, 102
death penalty. *See* capital punishment
Deer Lake, 125, 134
Deitch, Michele Y., 185
Denis, Yves, 151–52
Dennie, Heather, 173
deoxyribonucleic acid. *See* DNA
Deschênes, Jules, 164
Deslauriers, George, 82–83
Devitt, William, 128
Dhak, Sukh, 183
Dillinger, John, 54, 90
Dingman, Harold, 27
DNA, 119, 123–24
Don Jail, 36, 41, 105–7, *107*, 110–11, 160
    escapes from, 105–8
    new wing, 107
Donnelly, Richard, 71
Dorion, Frédéric. *See Special Public Inquiry 1964*
Down Inside (Clark), 42
Dr. Georges-L.-Dumont Regional Hospital, 117
Dr. Phil (TV show), 145
drones, 157
Drost, Ian L., 134
Drury, Bob, 140, 141, 143
Duhamel, Frédérik-Xavier, 173
Duhre, Sandip Singh, 182–83
Duke, Barry Kay, 49–50
Durocher, André, 162–65
Dzambas, Sreto "Lucky," 66, 67–68

Edmonton Institution, 120–21, 124

INDEX

Edmonton Journal, 53
Elseworth, Bert. *See* Cashel, Ernest
escapes from detention
   distance travelled after, 13, 20, 38, 60, 62, 68, 83, 110, 152, 165
   methods, 4
Estérel (Quebec), 149
Evening Journal, 11

Faïd, Rédoine, 156–57
Fandrich, Fred, 153–54
Fantino, Julian, 113
Farahbakhchian, Tony, 178, 184
Favreau, Guy, 163–64
Fawcett, Gordon, 128–29
Federal Bureau of Investigation (FBI), 36, 101, 179
Flam, Annie, 117
Flam, Nina, 117
Flying Bandit, The (Robertson), 53
Fogarty, Catherine, 59
Fond du Lac (Wisconsin), 140
Foran, John, 120
Foray, Sébastien, 147, 148–49
Forbes, 178
Ford, Robert Lee, 154
Forestall, Michelle Dorey, 64
Frontenac County Gaol, 40

Garrison, Randolph "Randy," 105–12
Gary (Indiana), 50
Gaspé region (Quebec), 83, 162
Gazoonie Gang, 129
Gazzana, Jennifer Lee. *See* Bembenek, Lawrencia "Laurie" Ann
Gazzana, Tony. *See* Gugliatto, Dominic
George, Tosin, 155
Giannini, Ted, 74
Global News, 133, 134
Globe, 11, 32, 72, 73, 78, 85, 117, 153, 166, 173, 175, 176
Globe and Mail, 18, 27, 38, 40, 41, 53, 55, 71, 84, 90, 99, 107, 113, 115, 117, 132, 149, 152, 164, 165, 171, 173
Go Boy! (Caron), 57
Goard, A.W., 67
Goi Hing Leung, 174–75

Gomke, Ron, 118
Goyer, Jean-Pierre, 85
Graham, Bob, 4
Grasse penitentiary (France), 155
Greece, 155, 181
Greenspan, Eddie, 114
Greenwood, Robin, 123
Grim Reapers, 121
Guardian, 156
Gugliatto, Dominic, 141–42

Hall, Terry, 133
hangman. *See* capital punishment
Hard Place to Do Time (Andersen), 126, 131
Hayes, Ernest Bruce. *See* Conn, Tyrone Williams "Ty"
Headingley Gaol (now Headingley Correctional Centre), 49–50, 52
Heed, Kash, 184
Helicopter escapes, 147–57
Hells Angels Motorcycle Club, 148, 152, 175
Hemingway, Ernest, 19–20, 41
Hertrich, Eddie, 102–3
Hirsh, Andre, 105–13
Honderich, Ted, 27–28
Honolulu Advertiser, 151
Hope (British Columbia), 153
Horenburger, Frederick, 145
hostages, taking of, 4, 57, 70–73, 78, 117–18, 122, 130, 156
Hudon-Barbeau, Benjamin, 148–50

Industrial School for Girls, 129
Inskip, Marnie, 140, 141, 143
Interpol, 87, 152, 164
Iran, 178

Jackrabbit Parole (Reid), 103
Jackson, Heather, 50
jail. *See* prison
Jeanjacquot, Sylvie, 90–91
Jenner, Brian, 151
Johnston, Shirley Ann, 122–23
Jones, Robert, 115
Journal de Montreal, Le, 86

Joyceville Institution, 58, 99–102
Jupp, Allan, 154

Kebezes, Louis, 137, 143
Kelly, Donald James, 69–79
Kennedy, John D., 37–38, *39*
Kennedy, Patrick, 38, 40
Kent Institution, 154–55
Kerby, G. E., 10, 15
Kingsley, Wilfred T., 21–22, 27
Kingston (Ontario), 5, 29, 32, 38, 43, 97, 101, 102–3
   as location for prisons, 58
Kingston Penitentiary, 2, 21–22, 27, 29–32, *31*, 33, 35, 43, 71, 84, 94, 126
   book about, 31
   closure, 32, 58
   escapes from, 17–18, 19, 22, 32, 38
   fire at, 17, 19
   prisoner transfer to Millhaven, 59
   riot, 57–59
Kingston Prison for Women, 99
Kingston Whig-Standard, 36, 38, 61, 63, 64, 67
Kingstonist, 64

L'instinct de mort (Mesrine), 82–83
La Santé Prison (Paris), 88–89, 155
Lacombe (North-West Territories, now Alberta), 7
Laentz, Michel, 83
Lake County Jail (Indiana), 51
Lakey, Jack, 141, 142
Lambert, Gaston, 62
Lane, William, 127
Larocque, Gerald, 66
Laurentian region (Quebec), 147, 150, 166
Lauzon, Ulysses, 33, *33*, 36–37
Laval (Quebec), 3, 84, 164, 165
Lavin, James, 69, 78
Laviolette, Mike, 184
Law, Deanna, 184
Leader-Post, 48, 54
Leavenworth Penitentiary, 102
Lebouthillier, Évelyn, 83
Leclerc, George, 49, 51

Lefebvre, Denis, 151–52
Legere, Allan Joseph, 115–124
Legislative Assembly (Quebec), 162
Leishman, William Kenneth "The Flying Bandit," 48, *52*, 53–55, 96, 169
Leonard, Michael, 99
Lewis, John, 24–25, *26*
Liberal Party, 21, 27, 153, 163, 165, 171
Liberation, 90
Lille (France), 156
Lindsay (Ontario), 112
Line of Fire (Butts), 86
Liquor Control Board (store), 23–25, *26*
Lisacek, Albert, 166
Lloyd, Wallace, 62
Locke, Hugh, 112
Lower Mainland Regional Correctional Centre. *See* Oakalla Prison Farm
Lunn, A.J., 45–46
Luynes penitentiary, 155
Lyrette, Marc, 175

Macdonald, W.L., 8–9
MacIntyre, Linden, 41
Mackin, Bob, 184
MacLean, Rick, 117
Maclean's, 27, 93
MacWilliams, Carol Ann "Corky," 69, 77–78
MacWilliams, Jack, 69
Malton Airport (now Pearson), 46
Manitoba, 46, 47
   police, 49
Maricopa County Jail (Arizona), 94
Marion (US Penitentiary), 94, 102
Marrocco, Frank, 143, 145
Maruya, Catherine, 110
Masse, Joseph, 162
McAteer, Steve, 111
McCaffrey, P.J., 64–66
McCauley, Thomas William, 59–60, 66
McCullough, Frank, 106–7
McDonald, Donald John "Mickey," 34, *34*, 36–37
McDougall, Fraser, 127
McKay, Bruce, 133
McMullen, Edward, 17, 20

INDEX

McSherry, Peter, 18, 20, 22, 27, 33–37
Mercer, Michelle, 118
Mercier, Jean-Paul, 84–87, 165–66
Mesrine, Jacques "Le grand gangster," 3, 83–90, 166
Metro Toronto Police. *See* Toronto police
Metropolitan Toronto West Detention Centre, 142
Miller, Theresa, 62–63
Millhaven Institution, 1, 3–4, 43, 58–59, 60, 62, 65, 94, 97, 103
   attempted escapes from, 98
   escapes from, 1, 4, 60, 61
   transfer of prisoners to, 59, 102
Milligan, Bernice, 64
Milwaukee (Wisconsin), 138, 146
Milwaukee Journal Sentinel, 138
Milwaukee Magazine, 140
Milwaukee Police Department, 138, 143
Minelli, Nicholas "Nick," *35*, 35–36
Ministry of Community Safety and Correctional Services (Ontario), 172–73
Ministry of Public Security (Quebec), 152, 173, 183
Minneapolis, (Minnesota), 20–21
Miramichi (New Brunswick), 115, 118, 120, 122
Miramichi Leader, 117
Mission Minimum Institution, 169, 171–72
mistaken releases, 172–75
Mitchell, Patrick Michael "Paddy," 95, 97–103
Moncton (New Brunswick), 116, 118
Monster of the Miramichi. *See* Legere, Allan Joseph
Mont-Tremblant (Quebec), 147
Montreal, 3, 19, 60, 82–83, 86–87, 152, 165, 182, 183
   police, 63, 66, 164
Montreal Detention Centre. *See* Bordeaux Prison
Montreal Gazette, 33, 87, 90, 132, 150, 153, 162
Montrose, Robert, 113
Mooney Mark 21, 50

Morris, Ralph Whitfield, 169–72
Mullins, H.A., 27
Murder on the Inside (Fogarty), 59
Musgrave, Susan, 103–4
Musgrave, Terrance "Terry" Derek, 105–12

Napanee (Ontario), 62, 65
National Parole Board, 53
National Post, 169
Nelson, Chris, 122
New Westminster Gaol, 126
Newbury, Raymond, 62
Newbury, William, 62
Newcastle (New Brunswick), 116–18
News Leader, 181
Niagara Regional Police, 66
Niagara-on-the-Lake (Ontario), 66
Nipissing, Lake, 71
North Bay (Ontario), 69, 72, 75
   police, 70, 71, 73
North Bay Jack Garland Airport, 70
North Bay Jail, 69–70
North Bay Police Commission, 72
North Fraser Pretrial Centre (NFPC), 178–80, 183, 185–86
North Shore Mountains, 125, 134
North York (Ontario), 109–11
North-West Mounted Police (NWMP), 8–10
North-West Territories (now Alberta), 7–11
Northern Daily, 181
Nuss, Rudolph, 3, 66, 68

O'Driscoll, John, 113
Oag, Donald, 65–66
Oag, James, 65
Oakalla Prison Farm, 125–26, *127*
   attempted break into, 131
   attempted escapes from, 126–27
   escapes from, 126, 129, 130, 132–33
   gallows, 128, 130
   granite staircase, 134, *135*
Oakland (California), 36
Office of the Correctional Investigator 2018–2019 Annual Report (Zinger), 122

Oklahoma State Penitentiary, 94
Ontario Provincial Police (OPP), 60, 62–63, 66–67, 71, 75, 78–79, 112
Opération Écrivisse, 152
Orsainville Zoo, 151
Ottawa (Ontario), 4, 35, 95
   airport, 96–98
Ottawa Citizen, 45, 47, 59, 96, 130
Ottawa Police, 184
Ottawa-Carleton Detention Centre, 98, 173
overcrowding in prisons, 42, 58, 106, 110, 130, 134, 147

Pal, Royhit Alvin, 178
Palmer, Robert, 113
Paquet, Marina, 151
Paris (France), 88, 155
   police, 90
Parkinson, Donald, 63
parole, 22, 27–28, 48, 53, 104, 141, 144, 150, 170–71, 182
Parti Québécois, 153
Pascagoula (Mississippi), 37
Payet, Pascal, 155–56
Peace Officers in Correctional Services of Quebec, 148
Pearson International Airport (Toronto), 97
Pearson, Lester B. (prime minister), 163
penal philosophy
   Auburn system, 29, 126
   Eastern State or Pennsylvania model, 88, 160
penitentiary. *See* prison
Pennycuick, Alick, 8–9, 14
Percé (Quebec), 83
Percé Jail, 83
physical punishment, 2, 31, 32
Pied-du-Courant prison, 159
Pitre, Marguerite Ruest, 161–62
Police Stories (Berrigan), 77
Pomerleau, Serge, 151–53
Port Coquitlam (British Columbia), 178, 185
Porte de Clignancourt (France), 90
Portsmouth Penitentiary, 19

prison
   features, 3
   jail and penitentiary, differences between, 2
   security levels, 58, 62
   See also escapes from detention
Prison d'Orsainville, 150, 152–53, 155
Prison for Women, 58
Prison Journal, 3
Provençal, Dany, 148–50
Province, 178
Purina Animal Hall of Fame, 74

Quanto's Law. *See Canadian Justice for Animals in Service Act*
Quebec City, 86–87, 151
Quebec Detention Centre. *See* Prison d'Orsainville
Quebec Superior Court, 153

Radclive, John Robert, 14–15
Réau prison, 156
Red Deer (North-West Territories, now Alberta), 8
Red Deer River, 7, 9
Red Lake (North-West Territories, now Alberta), 48, 53
Redmond, Mary Beatrice, 116
Reid, Stephen, 93–105, *100*
Renous (New Brunswick), 116
restraints, 11, 14, 21, 59, 94, 111, 117
reward, 11, 15, 32, 72, 117, 164, 185
Rigby (rancher), 13
Rivard, Lucien, 162–65
Riverdale Hospital, 106
Rives, Carmen, 89
Robertson, Heather, 53
Robins, Ira, 145
Robinson R44, 147, *149*, 151
Rogers, Leo, 71–72
Rose, Ian, 69, 78
Royal Canadian Mounted Police (RCMP), 38, 51, 117–18, 121, 131–32, 142, 154, 163, 178, 181, 183–84
Royal Commission of Inquiry (Drost Commission), 134

INDEX

Rutherford, Chris, 113
Ryan, Norman "Red," 17–25, *25*, 28, 29
Ryan, Russ, 27

Saint-Jérôme detention centre, 147–48, 155
Saint-Louis-de-Blandford (Quebec), 87
Saint-Pierre, Ernest, 87
Saint-Vincent-de-Paul Penitentiary, 3, 84, *85*, 86, 165–66
Sainte-Anne-des-Plaines (Quebec), 84, 119, 175
Sanders, G.E., 11, 15
Sarnia (Ontario), 23
  police department, 23–25, *26*
Sarnia Canadian Observer, 23
Saskatoon (Saskatchewan), 122
Saturday Star, 105
Schneider, Jeanne "Janou," 82–84
Schultz, Christine, 139, 145
Schultz, Elfred "Fred" O., 138–45
Schultz, Sean, 139–40
Schultz, Shannon, 139
Sedona (Arizona), 101
Select Committee (1831), 2–3
Sheppard, Leslie, 105–9, 114
Shook, Russ, 50
Silver, Ernest, 62
Silver, Steven E., 61–62, 66
Simpson, Gordon, 17
Singleton, John, 62
Skead (Ontario), 74
Smith, Henry, 31
Smith, James, 117
Smith, Richard "Buddy," 61–62
Special Public Inquiry 1964 (Dorion), 163
St. Onge, Dave, 5
Steinbach (Manitoba), 50
Stonehouse, Edward, 22–23, 27
Stonehouse, James, 23
Stony Mountain Penitentiary (now Stony Mountain Institution), 9, 48, 53
Stopwatch Gang, 4, 93, 101
Stopwatch Gang, The (Weston), 95, 101–2
Strapatsas, Simitrios, 175

Sudbury General Hospital, 75
Sullivan, Andrew, 17, 20
Sûreté du Québec (SQ), 84, 87, 152–53, 163, 166
Swackhamer, J.W., 58

Tahvili, Omid, 178, *179*, 180–81, 185–86
Taycheedah Correctional Institution, 140–43
Teolis, Tommasina, 161
Terre Haute (Indiana), 94
Tesher, Ellie, 114
Thériault, Lise, 153, 175
This Bank Robber's Life (Mitchell), 95
Thomas, D.A., 7
Thomas, David, 154
Thomas, Gwynne "Jocko," 22, 37
Thunder Bay (Ontario), 53–54, 137, 141–42, 145
Thunder Bay District Jail, 142
Ticket of Leave, 22
Ticne, Edwin, 180–81
Time, 21, 27
Toronto, 19–20, 41, 45, 47, 77, 109
  police, 106, 108–10, 112, 113
Toronto Daily Star, 19, 21, 22, 23, 24, 25, 27, 28, 37, 82
Toronto Jail. *See* Don Jail
Toronto Star, 4, 70, 71, 72, 73, 75, 106, 108, 109, 111, 113, 141, 175
Toronto Sun, 143, 144
tracker dogs, 60–61, 63–64, 66, 72, 77, 134
  See also Cloud II
Transair, 48

University of New Brunswick Allan Legere Digital Archive, 118
Urquhart, Howard, 38, 40

Vallée, Brian, 41
Vallée, Charles-Amédée, 159–60
Valley Helicopters, 153
Vancouver (British Columbia), 129, 131, 154, 183
Vancouver Daily World, 14

Vancouver Sun, 121, 128, 131, 180, 181, 183
Vanity Fair (magazine), 140, 143
Vaughan Street Jail (Winnipeg), 51–52, 54
Vaujour, Michel, 155
Vaujour, Nadine, 155
Veniot, André, 118
Vice, 148

Wagner, Claude, 162
Walsh, Matt, 19–20
Warkworth Institution, 94, 99
Washington Post, 137, 141, 142
Wasted Time (Hertrich), 103
Waterloo County Jail, 33
Webster, Jack, 133
Weekly News Record, 8, 15
West Vancouver, 66
Wetaskiwin Times, 13
What Happened to Mickey? (McSherry), 33–37
Wheaton, Don, 117

White, Jack, 116
Who Killed Ty Conn (MacIntyre and Burke), 41
Wilcox, Ellis, 127–28
Willsher, Kim, 156
Wilson, Kelly, 123
Windsor, Jimmy, 34
Winnipeg (Manitoba), 46–48, 50–52
Winnipeg International Airport, 48
Winnipeg Sun, 50, 51
Wisconsin, 137, 140, 143, 145
Woman on Trial (Bembenek), 138
Worthington, Peter John Vickers, 143–44
Wotherspoon, William, 71, 73
Wright, Lionel "The Ghost," 4, 95–103

Yardley, William, 64
York County Jail, *120*
Youth International Party "Yippies," 131

Zess, Judy, 138, 143
Zinger, Ivan, 122

ABOUT THE AUTHOR

Jen Ross Photography

LORNA POPLAK IS A TORONTO-BASED writer, editor, and researcher. Her background is in law, literature, information technology, and technical communications, and her written work has included historical and scientific articles, travel pieces, short fiction, and a radio play. Lorna's first two non-fiction books, both published by Dundurn Press, are *Drop Dead: A Horrible History of Hanging in Canada*, which examined the period between Confederation and the abolition of the death penalty in 1976, and *The Don: The Story of Toronto's Infamous Jail*, which focused on Toronto's landmark jail from its inception to the present day. In 2022, *The Don* was shortlisted for both the Crime Writers of Canada Excellence Award and the Heritage Toronto Book Award. Lorna is a member of Crime Writers of Canada, Sisters in Crime, and Mesdames of Mayhem. Further information may be found at www.lornapoplak.com.